KING ARTHUR

AND HIS KNIGHTS OF THE ROUND TABLE

Written by Roger Lancelyn Green

Teacher Guide

www.MemoriaPress.com

KING ARTHUR AND HIS KNIGHTS OF THE ROUND TABLE
Written by Roger Lancelyn Green

TEACHER GUIDE
Contributing Editors: Tanya Charlton, Caleb Kinlaw, Ashley Gratto

ISBN 978-1-61538-063-3

Cover illustration by Starr Steinbach

Contents

King Arthur

Discussion Questions Key

PREPARING TO READ:

REVIEW

- Orally review any previous vocabulary.
- Review the plot of the book as read so far.
- Periodically review the concepts of character, setting, and plot.

STUDY GUIDE PREVIEW

- Reading Notes:
  - Read aloud together
  - This section gives the student key characters, places, terms that are relevant to a particular time period, etc.
- Vocabulary:
  - Read aloud together so that students will recognize words when they come across them in their reading.
- Comprehension Questions:
  - Read through these questions with students to encourage purposeful reading.

READING:

- Student reads the chapter (or selection of the chapter for that lesson) independently or to the teacher (for younger students).
- For younger students, you can alternate between teacher-read and student-read passages. Model good reading skills. Encourage students to read expressively and smoothly. Teacher may occasionally take oral reading grades.
- While reading, mark each vocabulary word as you come across it.
- Have students take note in their study guide margin of pages where a comprehension question is answered.

AFTER READING:

VOCABULARY

- Look at each word within the context that it is used, and help your student come up with the best synonym that defines the word. (Make sure it is a synonym the student knows the meaning of.)
- Record the word's meaning in the students' study guides. (Use students' knowledge of Latin and other vocabulary to decipher meanings.)

COMPREHENSION QUESTIONS

- Older students can answer these questions independently, but younger students (2nd-4th) need to answer the questions orally, form a good sentence, and then write it down, using correct punctuation, capitalization, and spelling. (You may want to write the sentence down for the younger student after forming it orally, and then let the student copy it perfectly.)
- It is not necessary to write the answer to every question. Some may be better answered orally.
- Answering questions and composing answers is a valuable learning activity. Questions require students to think; writing a concise answer is a good composition exercise.

QUOTATIONS AND DISCUSSION QUESTIONS

- Use the Quotations and Discussion Questions section of each lesson as a guide to your oral discussion of the key concepts in the chapter that may not be covered in the comprehension questions.
- These talking points can take your oral discussion to a higher level than covered in the students' written work. Use this time as an opportunity to introduce higher-level thinking. You can introduce concepts the students may not be mature enough to fully understand yet but that would be beneficial for them to begin thinking about.
- A key to the Discussion Questions is in the back of the Teacher Guide.

ENRICHMENT

- The Enrichment activities include composition, copywork, dictation, research, mapping, drawing, poetry work, literary terms, and more.
- This section has a variety of activities in it, but the most valuable activity is composition. Your student should complete at least one composition assignment each week. Proof student's work and have student copy composition until grammatically perfect. Insist on clear, concise writing. For younger students, start with 2-3 sentences, and do the assignment together. The student can form good sentences orally as you write them down, and then the student copies them.
- These activities can be completed as time and interest allow. Do not feel you need to complete all of these activities. Choose the ones that you feel are the best use of your students' time.

UNIT REVIEW AND TESTS

- There is a unit review and a quiz or test following every few lessons (varies by individual guide).
- On the weeks that have these reviews and tests, you may want to do the review early in the week, and then drill it orally a couple of times before giving the test at the end of the week.
- A final comprehensive test is also included.

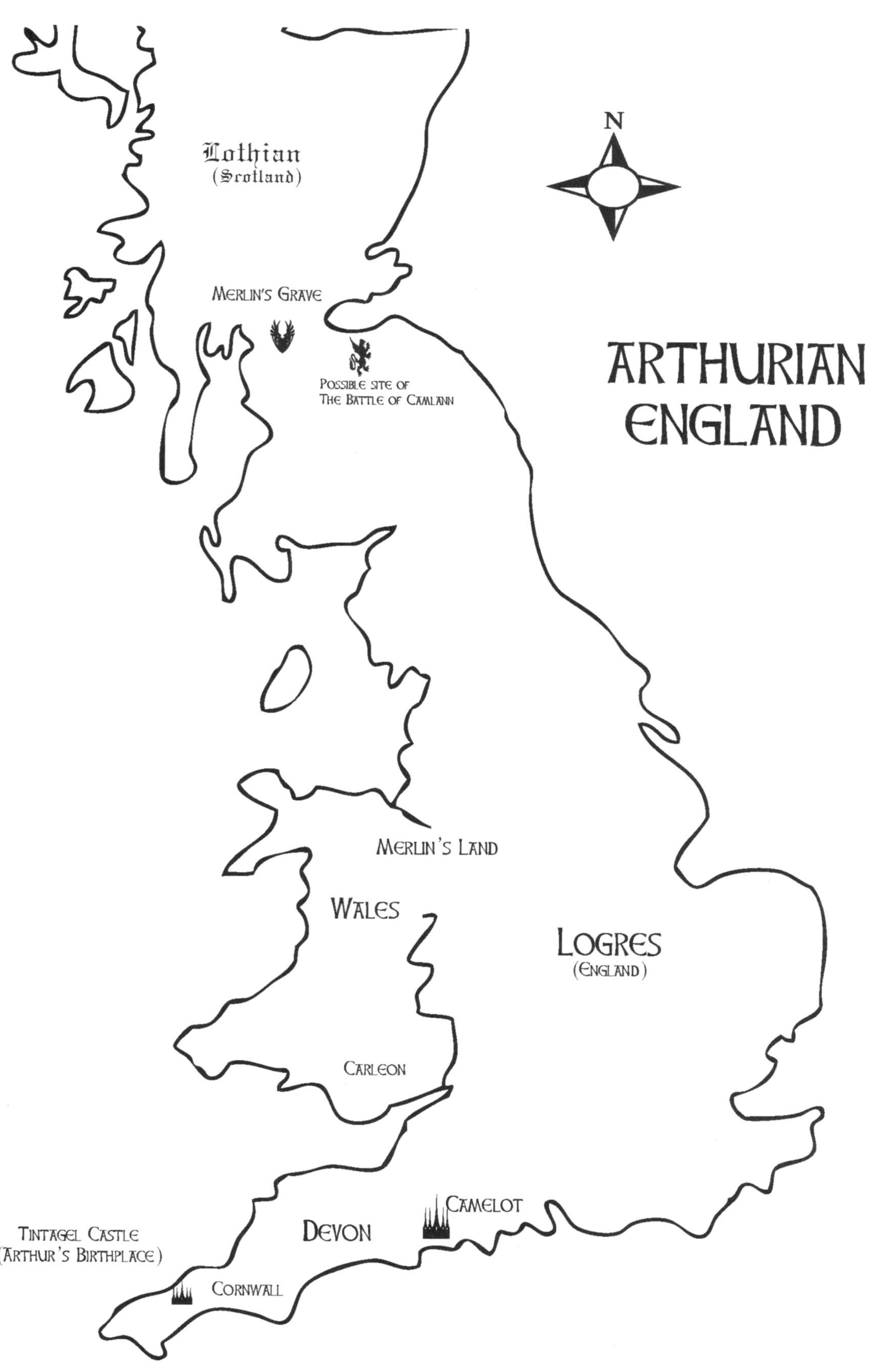
N
Lothian
(Scotland)
Merlin's Grave
Possible site of
The Battle of Camlann
ARTHURIAN
ENGLAND
Merlin's Land
Wales
Logres
(England)
Carleon
Camelot
Devon
Tintagel Castle
(Arthur's Birthplace)
Cornwall

About the Author: Roger Lancelyn Green

Roger Lancelyn Green (1918-1987) was a British author and academic. He wrote works in fiction as well as several biographies. He was a student of C. S. Lewis in Oxford and a member of the Inklings, a famous group of scholars who met to discuss ideas. Most of his fictional books focus on legend and mythology. Among the ten biographies he authored are three about Lewis Carroll, the writer of *Alice's Adventures in Wonderland.* Greene did not limit himself to writing books. He worked at a library in Oxford, taught classes at the University of Liverpool, and helped found the Lewis Carroll Society.

About the Illustrator: Lotte Reiniger

Charlotte (Lotte) Reiniger (1899-1981) was born in Germany and became fascinated with Chinese shadow puppetry as a child. Her early works of art contained silhouettes against elaborate backgrounds. Her drawings were well received in the art community, and she went on to study animation. She made short animated films which achieved popular success. The illustrations drawn for Green's *King Arthur* were made near the end of her artistic career. At the start of WWII, she and her husband fled Germany to London. She eventually returned to her homeland after the war.

About the Origins of the Legend:

King Arthur was said to have been a great warrior who lived during the 6th century at the time when the Romans were leaving Britain. Stories of his exploits survived for centuries by being passed down orally to each generation. Not until the 9th century does the first written word about Arthur appear. It was a single paragraph written in Latin about battles which Arthur fought. Later tales were developed in Brittany, France. The stories developed into French romances, and were added to and changed over the years. Sir Thomas Malory compiled the stories into the most well-known English version of the legend. His *Le Morte D'Arthur* (*The Death of Arthur*) was published in 1485 and has ever since been considered the definitive narrative of the King Arthur stories. Malory wrote the book in Newgate Prison, where he died soon after its completion.

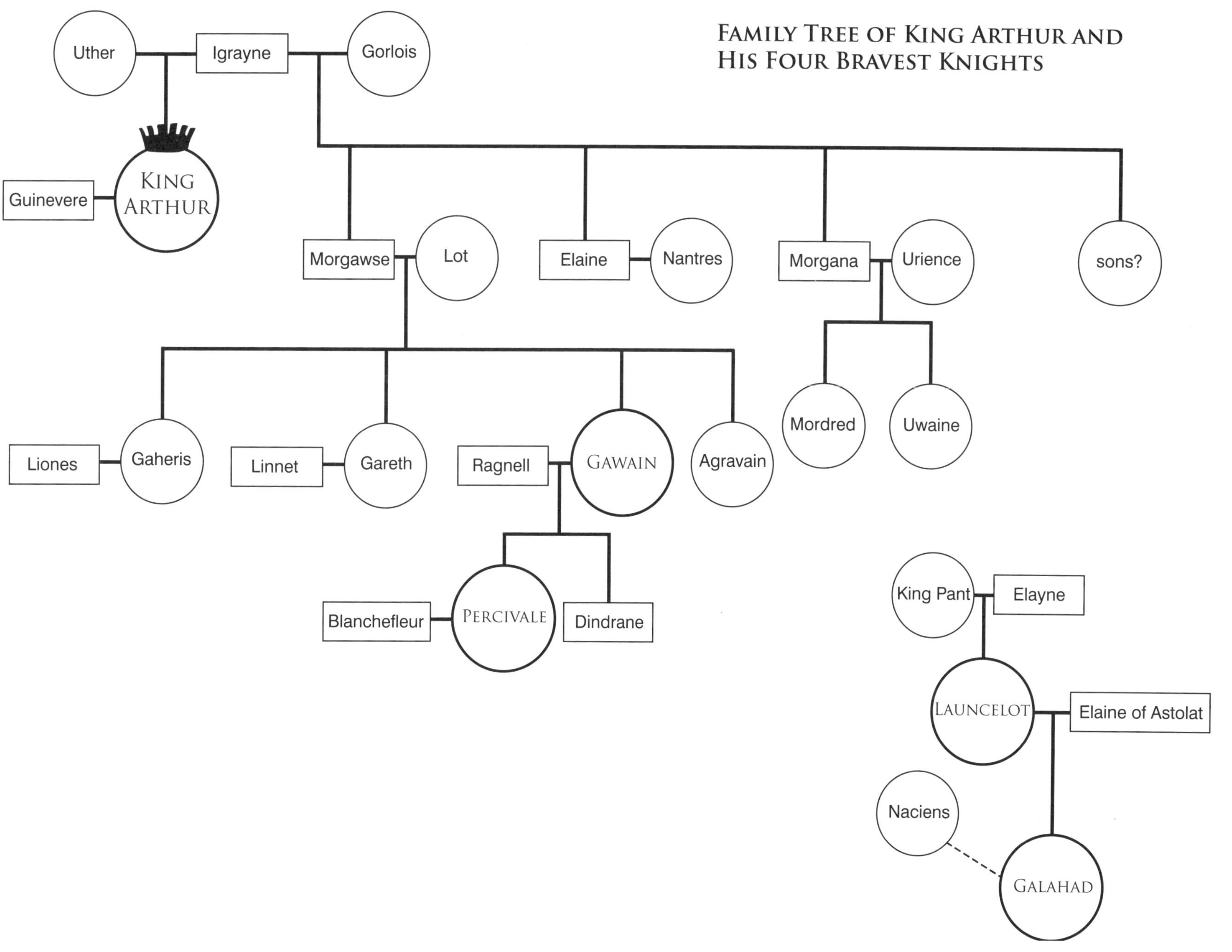

Family Tree of King Arthur and
His Four Bravest Knights
Uther
Igrayne
Gorlois
King Arthur
Guinevere
Morgawse
Lot
Elaine
Nantres
Morgana
Urience
sons?
Liones
Gaheris
Linnet
Gareth
Ragnell
Gawain
Agravain
Mordred
Uwaine
Blanchefleur
Percivale
Dindrane
King Pant
Elayne
Launcelot
Elaine of Astolat
Naciens
Galahad

"A little while after his birth at dark Tintagel, Uther, who hearkened to my words, gave the child into my care, and I bore him to Avalon, the Land of Mystery."

Reading Notes

Camelot	capital of Arthur's kingdom; modern-day Winchester, England
Uther Pendragon	king of Briton; father of Arthur
Igrayne	mother of Arthur; unfaithful wife of Gorlois
Avalon	Land of Mystery; place where Merlin took Arthur as an infant
Excalibur	Arthur's sword with magical scabbard
Logres (Lów-gris)	the name given to the land over which Arthur ruled
King Pellinore	killed knights for traveling on a road; nearly killed Arthur, and then began to chase the "Questing Beast"
Britons	a Celtic people inhabiting Britain before the time of the Roman invasion
Saxons	Germanic tribe that invaded Britain in the 5th and 6th centuries

Vocabulary

Write the meaning of each **bold** word or phrase.

1. set a rich **pavilion** over it ornate tent
2. bowing his head in **reverence** awe; respect
3. did **homage** to Arthur a ceremony by which a man acknowledged himself the vassal of a lord; special honor

Comprehension Questions

Answer the following in complete sentences.

1. Describe the state of Britain just before King Arthur claims the throne. Britain had never been in a worse condition. Knights were fighting among themselves, and the Saxons were conquering much of the land.
2. Where does Merlin take the baby Arthur, and what gifts does he receive there? Merlin takes him to Avalon. The fairies promise that Arthur will be the best knight, the greatest king in Britain, and that he will live a long time.
3. What is Arthur's first goal as king? He plans to drive the Saxons out of Britain.
4. What is King Pellinore doing that causes a problem? He sets up a pavilion by the road and kills any knight that passes.

5. How does Arthur come to possess Excalibur? Merlin takes Arthur to a lake. Arthur gets into a boat and takes the sword from a hand stretching out of the water.

6. Why is Arthur's scabbard worth more than his sword? While he wears the scabbard, Arthur will not die of blood loss.

Discussion Questions

1. Who said the quotation? Merlin To whom? angry kings and knights
2. Look at the picture on the page preceding Chapter 1 in your book. Who is in the picture? What castle is in the background? What is happening?
3. If you had to divide this chapter into two different parts, where would you divide it, and why?

Enrichment

1. Scholars debate the historicity of King Arthur. It is not implausible that a warlord led a successful uprising against barbarian settlers around 500 A.D. Perhaps that man was Arthur. There is no evidence that disproves such a thesis. Think of what evidence would convince you that the legends of Arthur are true or false. Write a paragraph explaining what such evidence would look like.

2. Write a summary of Arthur and Merlin's relationship. Why is it significant?

"Bury us, I pray you, in the same tomb, and write upon it that here lie two brothers who slew one another by mischance …"

Reading Notes

Balyn	knight who struck the Dolorous Stroke
Balan	brother of Balyn and the one Balyn loved most in the world
King Ryon	cruel king of N. Wales
Garlon	the invisible knight
King Pelles	king of Castle Carbonek; victim of the Dolorous Stroke
Holy Grail	the cup Jesus drank from at the Last Supper
Castle Carbonek	place where Holy Grail resided; place of Dolorous Stroke

Vocabulary

Write the meaning of each **bold** word or phrase.

1. You may **redeem** your honor ______ to pay off; to compensate for
2. the damsel made many **lamentations** ______ expressions of grief; mournings
3. more sweetly than the **plaintive** nightingale ______ sorrowful

Comprehension Questions

Answer the following in complete sentences.

1. List three mistakes Balyn makes.
   He cuts off the head of the Lady of the Lake.
   He strikes the "Dolorous Stroke."
   He kills his brother Balan.
2. Why does Balyn strike Pelles? King Pelles is about to kill him because he has murdered Garlon at the feast.
3. Why is it called the "Dolorous Stroke" when Balyn strikes Pelles? Balyn is not worthy to touch the Holy Lance.
4. What is special about the cup and spear in Castle Carbonek?
   The cup is the Holy Grail, and the spear was used to pierce Jesus' side.
5. How do the cup and the spear arrive in England? They are brought by Joseph of Arimathea.

6. What happens to King Pelles after the "Dolorous Stroke"? He lies at Castle Carbonek with a wound that will not heal until Galahad cures him.

Discussion Questions

1. Who said the quotation? Balan To whom? Lady of Castle
2. The Lady of the Lake is killed in Arthur's court. Arthur neither honors her request nor protects her from Balyn. Does this reveal a weakness in Arthur?
3. Who was Joseph of Arimathea? Is it possible that he took the Grail to Britain?

Enrichment

1. Read about the history of Britain below.

The Roman Legacy in Britain

Before the Romans reached the British Isles, the land was inhabited by a tribe called Britons, which were part of a larger tribe called Celts. The Romans first invaded the island in 55 B.C., when two Roman legions crossed the English Channel under the leadership of Julius Caesar. In 43 A.D. the emperor Claudius attacked the Celts again and gained full control of Southern England. The northern part of Britain was never fully subdued, and a tribe called the Picts would often descend to attack the Romans. In 122 A.D. the emperor Hadrian built a wall stretching 80 miles across the island to prevent these raids from occurring. For many years this marked the northern boundary of the Roman Empire. Near the end of their time in Britain, the empire was being weakened by repeated barbarian attacks. Troops were being withdrawn from the boundary provinces to protect Italy. The Romans remained in Britain until 410 A.D. The legacy of the Romans remains to this day. The cities of London, Manchester, and York were all founded by Romans. Britain was never the same after the Romans arrived. Among the many ways which they improved the island was the network of roads they built. There was once a famous saying: "All roads lead to Rome." This was actually true. All across Europe, wherever the Romans went, they built roads leading back to Rome. There were more than 50,000 miles of paved roads leading out from the city of Rome. Originally these were built to make it easier for troops to move from place to place. Some of the Roman roads are still used in Britain today.

"Yet I would that you loved another;
for by her very beauty shall come the end of Logres—"

"A knight without mercy is dishonoured:
but to kill a fair lady is shame unto the world's end!"

Reading Notes

Lady Nimue	magical woman; friend of Merlin's and King Arthur's
Gawain	nephew of Arthur; brave knight of the round table

Vocabulary

Write the meaning of each **bold** word or phrase.

1. that is the **Siege** Perilous ______ seat, chair
2. go out to **succour** gentlewomen ______ to aid, assist, relieve
3. we lay this **penance** upon you ______ contrition, remorse, regret

Comprehension Questions

Answer the following in complete sentences.

1. Why would this period of Arthur's reign be considered the "Golden Age" of Logres?
   He accomplishes his chief goal of driving out the Saxons. The book says, "In this way peace came to the whole island for a great many years."
2. What is the purpose of the round table? The purpose of the round table is to end the quarreling of the knights as to who would get the best seat.
3. What is the seat reserved for the best knight called? Siege Perilous
4. List the five demands made of all knights in the "Order of Chivalry."
   Do no outrage, murder, or cruel things.
   Fly from treason and dishonesty.
   Give mercy to those who seek it.
   Always give help to ladies.
   Do not fight in any quarrel that is not just and righteous.

Discussion Questions

1. Who said the first quotation? Merlin To whom? Arthur
2. Who said the second quotation? four armed knights To whom? Gawain
3. The feasts at Camelot are held on Christian holidays such as Pentecost and Easter. Does this give us insight into the type of kingdom over which Arthur was ruling?
4. Why do you think Arthur chooses to marry Guinevere even after Merlin tells him that she will bring an end to Logres?

Enrichment

1. On a separate sheet of paper, answer the following questions:
   Why is it necessary to have rules for the knights?
   Which rules do you think would be the hardest to follow? Why?
   Do the knights in this chapter adhere to the chivalric code? Give examples.

Knights and Chivalry

Knights were men trained to fight on horseback. Kings and lords would use knights to fight for them and protect their castles from being attacked. In the early Middle Ages, knights were chiefly interested in extending their own estates. Often knights would treat peasants with disdain, killing people for personal gain. The church humanized and civilized the warrior instinct; it did not destroy or condemn it, but rather Christianized and elevated it. Gradually there developed a code of conduct which channeled the energy of warriors towards noble ends. This "code of conduct" was called *chivalry*. Chivalry demanded that the knight give all his efforts to serving three things: his lord, the Christian faith, and the lady he loved. Knights went through rigorous training, which began when they were just boys. A boy could become a page at the age of seven and train for seven years. Then he would become a squire for another seven years. If he had enough skills after fourteen years of training, he would be dubbed a knight.

"For though I lack a weapon, yet shall I lack no honour—
and if you slay me weaponless, it is you who will be shamed."

"I have loved her long, and she me. And I promised to fight
and slay whom she would, even though it were Arthur the King."

Reading Notes

King Pant and Elayne	king and queen of N. Wales; parents of Launcelot
Sir Accolon	Arthur's knight who loves Morgana le Fay
King Urience	husband of Morgana
Sir Uwaine	son of Morgana and Urience

Vocabulary

Write the meaning of each **bold** word or phrase.

1. **taunted** Sir Accolon ridiculed; provoked
2. Yield you to me as **craven** cowardly
3. her evil **purged** away purified, absolved, cleansed

Comprehension Questions

Answer the following in complete sentences.

1. What is the last advice Merlin has for Arthur? He advises him to take good care of Excalibur and the scabbard.
2. What does Merlin say Launcelot's son will be named? Galahad
3. Where does Merlin go? He goes with Nimue to North Wales, where she puts a spell on him. He descends into a tomb, and the earth covers over him.
4. Why does Arthur not accept Sir Accolon's offer to spare his life during the fight? Arthur has taken vows not to admit cowardice, for to do so would be dishonorable.
5. What happens to Excalibur's scabbard? Morgana steals it while Arthur sleeps. She then throws it into a lake, where it sinks.

6. What is Morgana's peace offering to Arthur? She sends a servant bearing a mantle which will supposedly protect its wearer from harm. In truth, it burns anyone who puts it on.

Discussion Questions

1. Who said the first quotation? Arthur To whom? Sir Accolon
2. Who said the second quotation? Sir Accolon To whom? Arthur
3. This is not the first time that two knights have mistakenly fought to the death. It seems that if two knights lack their own shields and have visors down, then they are at risk of killing even a family member. Can you think of a way that such tragedies could have been avoided?
4. Why do you think Arthur would rather "die a hundred times" than to admit that he was beaten and cowardly?

Enrichment

1. Find examples in this chapter of characters adhering to the code of chivalry. Write these down on a separate sheet of paper.

   Possible answers: Accolon fighting for Morgana; Accolon offering Arthur a chance to yield before killing him; Arthur refusing to back out of battle even though he is weaponless; Arthur refusing to kill Accolon when he was defenseless

2. Copy the ninth paragraph of Ch. 4 beginning "At length they came to the place appointed … ." Notice spelling and punctuation.

   At length they came to the place appointed, and there under the shadow of a fair white hawthorn covered in flowers Nimue sat down, and Merlin laid his head upon her lap. Then, singing and playing, she wove a great magic round about him in nine circles, round Merlin and round the hawthorn bush. Merlin slept, and woke again: and now it seemed to him that he dwelt in the fairest tower in the world and the most strong. 'Lady,' he said, 'you have taken from me all my magic, so that never may I come out of this tower. Stay but with me, and leave me not alone in these enchantments.'

"As for the lace, you hid it but for love of your life—
and that is a little sin, and for it I pardon you."

Reading Notes

Sir Bernlak Knight of the Lake; the Green Knight

Vocabulary

Write the meaning of each **bold** word or phrase.

1. some **dire** enchantment it must be urgent, fearful
2. I heard of the fame and **valour** of your court heroism, courage
3. laughed aloud in **mockery** ridicule, derision

Comprehension Questions

Answer the following in complete sentences.

1. What is the challenge posed by the Green Knight, and who accepts it? If any man is brave enough to exchange stroke for stroke, the Green Knight will give him an axe. Sir Gawain accepts the challenge.

2. What is the agreement made between Sir Gawain and his host at the castle? The host will give Gawain what he kills while hunting, and Gawain will give the host what he receives that day in the castle.

3. What does Gawain receive from the lady of the castle? What does he keep hidden from the lord of the castle? She gives him kisses each day. She also gives him a green lace from her belt. Gawain does not tell his host about the green lace.

4. Why does the Green Knight wound Gawain rather than kill him? Gawain has not been honest with the lord of the castle. According to their agreement, he should have given the lord the lace from his wife's belt, but he keeps it secret, and it protects him.

5. Who is the Green Knight? He is the lord of the castle, Sir Bernlak.

6. What enabled him to live after being beheaded? Lady Nimue put magic on him.

Discussion Questions

1. Who said the quotation? Sir Bernlak To whom? Gawain
2. In the legends, many battles took place in which a knight refused to submit to his opponent even though he was defeated. Such knights appear to have valued their honor more than life itself. Gawain acted differently. Though he did not yield to the Green Knight, he kept a secret lace which protected him from harm. Do you think his behavior was honorable?
3. Gawain's discreet possession of a magic lace is similar to King Arthur's scabbard. Each item protected its bearer from being killed. The chivalric code placed upon all knights the requirement of being honest at all times. Neither Gawain nor Arthur told their opponents of their secret protection. Is this honest? Does it conflict with the chivalric code?

Enrichment

1. Read about medieval castles, and then draw a picture of Sir Bernlak's castle.

Features of a Medieval Castle

In the legend of Arthur, castles are depicted as elaborate stone structures. In fact, the castles of South West England in the 6th century were called *hill forts*. Hill forts were defensive barraks made of wood on a hill. Eventually the architecture of castles grew into the great stone structures we picture.

Here are some of the features of large stone castles:

outer curtain - outermost wall around the castle
outer gate - a gate in the outer curtain
drum towers - round fortresses built on the corners
moat - deep ditch which may have been filled with water
inner curtain - a second wall behind the outer curtain; thicker and stronger than the outer curtain
inner gate - a gate on the inner curtain
gatehouse - fortified section of inner curtain surrounding the gate; portcullis located here
murder holes - small slits from which castle defenders could ward off attackers at the gate
inner ward - a large open courtyard in the center of the castle
keep (tower) - a tall structure that served as a lookout as well as fortress; strongest part of a castle; if an enemy could break into the keep, the castle was effectively overtaken

"Merlin has spoken his name to you—and see, that name grows in letters of gold upon the empty siege on the right hand of the Siege Perilous!"

Reading Notes

Mordred	son of Morgana le Fay; Arthur's nephew
Sir Turquyn	evil knight
Lionel	Launcelot's cousin
Hector	Launcelot's half-brother
Allewes	evil sorceress; companion of Morgana le Fay

Vocabulary

Write the meaning of each **bold** word or phrase.

1. the **peerless** knight of whom Merlin had spoken unequalled
2. **bestow** upon him the high order of knighthood to confer, place
3. on the right hand of the Siege **Perilous** dangerous, risky

Comprehension Questions

Answer the following in complete sentences.

1. What kind of enchantment does Morgana le Fay place upon the sleeping Launcelot? Why?
   He will be put to sleep for seven hours so that she can take him to her dungeon.
2. Why does Launcelot choose the dungeon over one of the four women?
   They are false enchanters and it will dishonor his vows.
3. a) What bargain does Launcelot make with Morgana's servant?
   The bargain is to fight for her father (Bagdemagus) in return for his freedom.

   b) Why does she cry after she releases him? She is in love with him.
4. Launcelot faces three perils at the Chapel Perilous before he can come safely away with the sword and cloth. Name them:
   30 great black knights
   moving floor (earthquake)
   Sorceress Allewes wants a kiss
5. How does Launcelot get rid of the sorceress? He crosses himself.

Discussion Questions

1. Who said the quotation? Lady Nimue To whom? Arthur
2. How can a knight heal someone by simply touching the person? Does this mean that knights have special powers?
3. Many prophesies were made regarding the pending destruction of Logres. Why did Arthur and his knights fail to discuss how they could preserve Logres? What type of strategy might they have devised?

Enrichment

1. Draw a picture of the wounded man brought into Arthur's court at the beginning of this chapter.
2. Copy the paragraph in which Launcelot responds to the four Queens who have him imprisoned. It begins: "A hard choice indeed … ." Notice spelling and punctuation.

   "A hard choice indeed," said Launcelot, "to die or to choose one of you to be my love … Yet it is easily answered: I would rather die than shame my honour and my vows of knighthood. I will have none of you—for you are all false enchanters! As for Queen Guinevere, I will prove it in battle with any man alive that she is the truest lady to her lord of any living!"

"When you are a noble knight of noble birth,
you shall have my love—but not before!"

Reading Notes

Sir Gareth	brother of Gawain, Gaheris, and Agravaine; Knight of the Kitchen
Lady Linnet	damsel in distress; needed aid of Arthur's knights
Lady Liones	sister of Lady Linnet; practiced evil magic
Sir Ironside	Red Knight; under spell of Morgana le Fay
Castle Dangerous	name of castle Red Knight is besieging; home of Lady Liones

Vocabulary

Write the meaning of each **bold** word or phrase.

1. and of nobler **ancestry** than you are lineage
2. It's only a **wretched** kitchen knave miserable, woeful
3. uncourteous so to **rebuke** me and mock at me to reprove, criticize

Comprehension Questions

Answer the following in complete sentences.

1. What name does Sir Kay give to the strange knight? Beaumains
   Why? It means "Fair Hands," which suggests he has lazy, idle hands.

2. What are the three gifts Beaumains asks Arthur to grant him at the next Pentecost?
   He asks for meat and drink for one year.
   He asks to be granted the adventure of the damsel.
   He asks to be knighted by Launcelot.

3. What kind of help does the damsel need?
   She needs to have her sister rescued from being besieged by the Red Knight.

4. What is Lady Linnet's reaction after Beaumains slays the Black Knight?
   She accuses him of slaying him by treachery.

5. Why does Lady Linnet begin to think Gareth may be of noble birth?
   She is surprised that he defends her even though she insults him continuously.

Discussion Questions

1. Who said the quotation? Lady Liones To whom? Sir Gareth
2. Why do you think Sir Gareth puts up with Lady Linnet for so long? Do you think Sir Gareth behaves honorably to Lady Linnet? Would you have done likewise?
3. Is there a lesson to be learned in this story? What do you think it is?

Enrichment

1. Romances were stories and poems which always shared common elements. Some of these elements were: a) noble, idealized heroes, b) gallant love, c) adventure, d) code of honor, e) daring deeds, f) faraway settings, and g) fantastic events. Find an example of each element in this chapter and write it down on a separate sheet of paper. Answers will vary.
2. Write a paragraph explaining why you think Gareth wanted to conceal his identity.

"Only Launcelot bowed his head in his hands, and the tears ran between his fingers as he thought of his own love for Guinevere."

Reading Notes

King Rivalin	father of Tristram; king of Lyonesse
Morgan the Wicked	killer of Rivalin and usurper of his throne
Rual	servant of Rivalin who raised Tristram
King Mark	king of Cornwall; Tristram's uncle
King Gurman	king of Ireland; father of Iseult
Sir Marhault	King Gurman's knight; uncle of Iseult; slain by Tristram
Tintagel	King Mark's castle in Cornwall; castle where Igrayne was tricked by Uther

Vocabulary

Write the meaning of each **bold** word or phrase.

1. **restrain** the tears from running down their cheeks to hold back
2. kindly and lovingly **fostered** encouraged, nurtured, cared for
3. the wound **festered** became infected, rotted, decayed

Comprehension Questions

Answer the following in complete sentences.

1. How does Tristram arrive at the court of King Mark? He is kidnapped by a merchant. In a great storm, the merchant drops him off in Cornwall.
2. Why does Tristram go to Ireland the first time? His wound from the fight with Marhault will not heal. Only Iseult's mother can heal it, so he sails to Ireland under disguise to receive treatment.
3. Why does Tristram go to Ireland the second time? He plans on winning the goodwill of King Gurman so that King Mark might marry his daughter Iseult and thus establish peace.
4. What is the prize for killing the dragon in Ireland? The man who kills the dragon will get to marry Iseult.

5. How does Iseult discover Tristram's true identity? She matches the piece of metal from Marhault's head with the missing piece from Tristram's sword.

6. Why do they not marry? It is the honorable thing to do.

7. What would happen if they got married? There would be war between Cornwall and Ireland.

8. Why is Tristram banished from Cornwall? King Mark discovers that Iseult and Tristram are meeting in secret in the woods.

Discussion Questions

1. Read the quotation. Why does Launcelot cry? After hearing his story, Launcelot knows exactly how Tristram feels.
2. Siege Perilous, along with the neighboring chairs, is reserved for very brave knights. Does this hierarchy of seats defeat the purpose of the round table?
3. This legend was influenced by other famous stories and myths. Did any part of this story remind you of another story you've heard?

Enrichment

1. Write the lay of Tristram and Iseult in your own words.

2. The story of Tristram and Iseult revolves around the conflict of romantic love and political loyalty. Iseult had promised to marry King Mark, but she was in love with Tristram. Do you think she did the right thing in keeping her promise to King Mark? Write your answer on a separate sheet of paper.

"I have no lady. And yet … there is none fairer that ever I have seen than this damsel your daughter, the lady Enid …"

Reading Notes

Duke Yder	Duke Liconal's nephew and rightful heir of dukedom
Duke Liconal	knight who withheld nephew's inheritance from him
Sir Oringle	evil knight

Vocabulary

Write the meaning of each **bold** word or phrase.

1. hangs his head so **pensively** thoughtfully, contemplatively
2. great **desolate** valley of bare stones deserted, isolated
3. A vile **churl** this dwarf is a crude, ill-bred person
4. or her **rash** and cruel words reckless, careless

Comprehension Questions

Answer the following in complete sentences.

1. What does Guinevere want to do for Geraint? She wants to find him a maiden.
2. Why does Geraint want to joust with Duke Yder? It is Duke Yder's dwarf that strikes Geraint and Guinevere's damsel with a whip. He seeks revenge.
3. Who does Geraint take to the tournament? He takes Duke Liconal's daughter, Enid.
4. Why doesn't Geraint accept Duke Yder's invitation to his castle? He is not yet a knight and wants to seek adventures by himself.
5. Why does Geraint tell Enid not to speak to him on their journey in the woods? She insults him when she finds out that he is not a knight, and he is angry with her.
6. After Geraint is waylaid in the forest, Enid is abused by Sir Oringle. How does Geraint avenge this injustice? He wakes from his swoon and then chops off Sir Oringle's head.

Discussion Questions

1. Who said the quotation? Geraint To whom? Duke Liconal

Enrichment

1. Read about jousting below.

Jousting

Jousts allowed knights to show off their skills to others. The contestants fought on horseback with lances. They would also fight on the ground with swords. The goal was to hit your opponent off of his horse with a single blow. If you broke your lance on your opponent's shield, you received points. Lances could have either blunt or sharp ends. *Jousts of peace* involved blunted lances, but *jousts of war* involved the pointed deadly lances. Knights aimed for their opponent's head because it nearly always knocked them off their horse. Even a blunt lance could break the bones of an opponent. To be knocked off a horse running at full speed frequently resulted in broken necks and backs. Horses sometimes collided as well, resulting in injuries on both sides. A low wall was placed between the paths of the horses to prevent collisions. Jousting was so popular that special armor was designed specifically for the sport. Shields had slots on the sides in which the knights could rest their heavy lance when it was lowered. A "frog-mouthed" helmet was made with an eye slit so thin that the knight could see only by leaning his head down. At the moment of impact, he straightened his head and protected his face.

"This is devil's work!"

"By this your choice—to leave the choice to me—
you have undone the enchantment forever ..."

Reading Notes

Gromer Somer Joure	the giant knight who struck fear into anyone who approached; cursed by Morgana le Faye
Lady Ragnell	sister of Gromer Somer Joure; under the curse of Morgana; marries Gawain

Vocabulary

Write the meaning of each **bold** word or phrase.

1. her face grew pale and **indistinct** vague, hazy, murky
2. with a cry of **anguish** torment, distress, agonizing pain
3. low sweet voice **tremulous** with love trembling, quivering

Comprehension Questions

Answer the following in complete sentences.

1. What happens when King Arthur charges at Gromer Somer Joure? His horse stops in its tracks, his arms sink to his sides, and he is filled with great fear.
2. What quest does Gromer give to King Arthur? He tells Arthur to ask all the women he meets what it is that women most desire. After a year and one day, Arthur is to return and give his answer.
3. How do Gawain and Arthur react upon first seeing Lady Ragnell? Gawain turns pale and Arthur crosses himself.
4. In exchange for what does Ragnell tell King Arthur the answer to the riddle? She wants to marry one of Arthur's knights.
5. What is the correct response to the question that King Arthur has to answer? Women most want to rule over men.
6. What happens when Gawain kisses Ragnell? Ragnell turns into a beautiful lady.

7. Of what curse does Ragnell speak after they kiss? Morgana has cursed her to be ugly for twelve hours a day and pretty for the other twelve.

8. How does Gawain break the curse? He can choose when Ragnell will be pretty, but he gives the choice to her, which breaks the curse.

9. Rumor had it that Lady Ragnell later fled into the woods and gave birth to whom? Percivale

Discussion Questions

1. When was the first quotation spoken? when Arthur charged Gromer
2. Who said the second quotation? Ragnell To whom? Gawain
3. Why do you think Morgana le Fay keeps trying to kill Arthur?

Enrichment

1. Before going out to fight Gromer, King Arthur calls for his sword Excalibur and Ron his spear. Write a list of five things which King Arthur possesses. Give each possession a name that you think would be appropriate. Then write a paragraph about King Arthur using all these objects in an adventure, using the names you chose for them. The class will then try to guess each object.

2. Read the poem "The Wooing of Sir Keith" in the Appendix of this guide. Practice reading this poem aloud, and then recite it before an audience, putting all the drama and humor into your voice. This also makes a fun group performance if acted out.

"In the days long past Merlin the good enchanter told me that you would come when the highest moment of the realm of Logres drew near."

Reading Notes

Sir Gonemans Percivale's tutor in the art of knighthood

Blanchefleur Percivale's love

Vocabulary

Write the meaning of each **bold** word or phrase.

1. a couch of rich silk and **samite** silken cloth
2. robber whom you have slain so **valiantly** bravely, courageously
3. Percivale looking **scornfully** at Sir Kay contemptuously, disdainfully

Comprehension Questions

Answer the following in complete sentences.

1. What does Percivale have to do for Arthur to knight him? He has to bring back his goblet and the Red Knight's armor.
2. How does Percivale respond when Arthur tells him he needs arms and weapons? He says that he has a dart and will go and get the golden armor.
3. Who is the damsel in the strange castle? Lady Blanchefleur
4. What does Percivale get to see in the castle? He sees a damsel carrying a grail (covered), a damsel carrying a plate, and a damsel carrying a spear dripping with blood.
5. When does Blanchefleur tell Percivale he will see the Holy Grail again? He will see it when it comes to Logres (when Galahad sits in the Siege Perilous).
6. Who does Blanchefleur say will be the downfall of Logres? Launcelot
7. Why does Percivale leave Blanchefleur? He wants to pursue the quest for the Holy Grail.

Discussion Questions

1. Who said the quotation? Arthur To whom? Percivale
2. Do you find it hard to believe that a boy who grew up in the woods could defeat a trained knight with a dart?
3. Does Percivale's defeat of the knight in golden-red armor remind you of a Bible story?

Enrichment

1. Read about medieval weapons below.

Medieval Weapons

A *halberd* was a heavy axe weapon with a long staff handle. It had a hook behind the axe blade used to trip horses or pull knights from their saddles. A *pollax* was a weapon used by foot soldiers. It was a long wooden pole with a metal spear point on the end. It also had an axe blade below the spear point, and on the back of the axe was a blunt hammer. This was used to strike at the opponent's head. *Caltrops* were small iron spike balls which were scattered on a battlefield to maim the feet of enemy horses. When placed on the ground they always had at least one spike pointing upward. *Longbows* were six feet high and could shoot arrows up to 1000 feet. A thin metal tip called a *bodkin* was designed to pierce through armor. A *mace* was a stick with a grooved metal head. A stick with an iron ball attached to a chain was called a *flail*.

"Alas! I have lived too long, for now I am dishonoured!"

Reading Notes

Dolorous Lady	imprisoned in scalding water by Morgana le Fay
Elaine of Astolat	daughter of King Pelles; in love with Launcelot

Vocabulary

Write the meaning of each **bold** word or phrase.

1. to seek **redress** for the wrongs amends
2. less and less cause to prove their **prowess** skill, aptitude
3. Elaine **prospered** not at all in her love succeeded

Comprehension Questions

Answer the following in complete sentences.

1. Why does King Arthur feel no jealousy towards Launcelot and Guinevere?
He trusts them.
2. What is the first sign of evil creeping into Logres in this time of great peace and strength?
Launcelot and Guinevere are spending more and more time together without the knowledge of Arthur.
3. Who does Launcelot find at the Castle Carbonek? He finds King Pelles.
4. Who is Pelles' ancestor? His ancestor is Joseph of Arimathea.
5. What does Launcelot see when he sits down at the table with Pelles?
He sees the Grail procession (spear, platter, cup).
6. What does Pelles tell Launcelot is special about the cup besides the fact that Jesus drank out of it?
It was used to catch the blood of Jesus after his side was pierced.
7. Why does Launcelot feel he is so dishonored that he goes insane? He marries Elaine thinking she is Guinevere. This is a betrayal of Arthur because he thinks Elaine is the wife of his king, and a betrayal of his love for Guinevere because he married another woman.
8. What does Sir Bors find when he gets to the Castle Carbonek? He finds Elaine and Launcelot's newborn son, Galahad.

Discussion Questions

1. Who said the quotation? Launcelot
2. After professing his love to the wrong woman, Launcelot goes mad because he feels dishonored. What do you think honor means? Why do you think it was so important to knights? Is it important to people today?

Enrichment

1. Draw a picture of Launcelot after losing his mind.
2. Write a paragraph summarizing this chapter.

3. Read the poem "The Lady of Shalott" in the Appendix of this guide. How does it differ from the story as told by Green? What are the similarities?

   *If you have the Memoria Press *Poetry for the Grammar Stage*, this is a good time to do the lesson on this poem.

"Sir, this is not my sword, nor am I worthy to wear it at my side. Evil shall come to any who seeks to draw it knowing that he is not worthy …"

Reading Notes

Naciens hermit who raised Galahad

Vocabulary

Write the meaning of each **bold** word or phrase.

1. All that night Galahad kept his **vigil** watch, surveillance
2. but in their **stead** a new inscription place, position
3. I shall go forth in quest of the Holy **Grail** cup of Jesus

Comprehension Questions

Answer the following in complete sentences.

1. Who does Launcelot find when the fair lady on the white horse takes him to an abbey?
   He finds Galahad, Sir Bors, and Sir Lionel.
2. What does the lady ask Launcelot to do?
   She asks him to knight Galahad.
3. What is seen floating down the river?
   A stone is seen with a sword stuck in it.
4. Why does Launcelot refuse to attempt to remove the sword from the stone?
   He knows that he is not worthy.
5. What does the coming of Galahad to Arthur's court signify?
   Logres will end in one year.
6. What is the history of the sword Galahad pulls from the stone?
   It is the sword that Balyn used to kill his brother Balan.
7. Who hides his face when the Holy Grail comes through Arthur's court?
   Mordred hides his face.
8. Why do Arthur's knights leave him?
   They go to seek the Holy Grail.

Discussion Questions

1. Who said the quotation? Launcelot To whom? Arthur
2. Upon taking the sword from the stone, Galahad declares, "Now have I the sword that struck the Dolorous Stroke." Is this true? Why does he say this?
3. The vision of the Holy Grail shared among all the knights is described as filling each man with the joy and peace of God. The knights consider the vision unsatisfactory and vow to not only view the Grail, but to touch it as well. Why do you think they take the vision as a challenge to find the Grail?
4. Why do you think the knights pursue the Grail in groups of twos and threes rather than staying together?

Enrichment

1. Read about the Holy Grail below.
2. How do you think a dinner bowl (graal) eventually became the Holy Grail? Write your answer on a separate sheet of paper.

The Holy Grail

In the early legends, the *graal* was not a cup but a bowl which was placed on the dinner table to hold food or drink. The graal gradually became what we read of today, as different writers gave their own versions of the legend. Chretien de Troyes wrote of the graal as a flat dish (graal comes from *gradal*, a dish brought to the table). Chretien's tale is the oldest story in which the knights encounter a magical graal, but he did not explain why or how the graal held magical powers. After Chretien died, another writer changed the story further. Robert de Boron called the graal a chalice. This was the chalice from which Jesus drank and was later used to catch his blood when he was taken down from the cross. De Boron also added the story of Joseph of Arimathea taking the Holy Grail to Britain.

"Now blessed be the good fortune that brings this shield to me."

"I give you my word that never again will I feel envy towards Sir Galahad."

Reading Notes

White Knight keeper of the shield that belongs to Galahad

Vocabulary

Write the meaning of each **bold** word or phrase.

1. **clad** all in shining white armor clothed
2. I am a **hermit** one who lives in solitude
3. make you a knight **forthwith** immediately

Comprehension Questions

Answer the following in complete sentences.

1. What will the magical shield do for the one who wears it? The shield will bring the wearer ill fortune within three days. It will also help the wearer in the quest for the Grail.
2. Whom is the shield for? It is for the best knight.
3. Who takes the shield first, and what is the result? King Bagdegamus takes the shield and is smitten by the White Knight.
4. What does the White Knight tell Galahad concerning the history of the shield? Made in the Holy Land, the shield was brought by Joseph of Arimathea to Britain. The cross was painted with his blood.
5. For which two vices does the hermit wound Sir Melyas? The hermit wounds Sir Melyas for pride and greed.
6. Why is Percivale angry at Galahad? Galahad had knocked him off of his horse.
7. What happens when Percivale is attacked by twenty knights? Galahad appears and saves his life.

8. Evil spirits disguised as a horse and lady try to hinder Percivale on his quest. How does he save himself from them? He crosses himself.

9. Who takes Percivale to the Enchanted Ship at the end of Chapter 3? Didrane, his sister, takes him to the ship.

Discussion Questions

1. Who said the first quotation? Galahad To whom? the squire
2. Who said the second quotation? Percivale To whom? the hermit
3. Why do you think Sir Galahad chooses to take the easy path rather than the challenging path? Is there honor in that?
4. The lady who tempts Percivale to betray his oath made to Blanchefleur is obviously trying to ruin his quest. The black horse, however, seems to help Percivale in his quest. Why do you think the horse, which is a demon, helps Percivale?

Enrichment

1. In Chapter 3 Percivale needed to distinguish what was real from what was an evil spirit. Now you will try to distinguish between what is true and what is false. For this activity you will need a partner. One student will tell the other student three true statements about these two chapters and one false statement. The other person must identify which one is false. The person trying to guess which one is a lie cannot look in their book. Take turns putting forward four statements and then guessing.

"Go forward in the fear of God, and live to tell of the ending of the quest of the Holy Grail …"

"Alas, all my great deeds of arms have I done for the sake of Queen Guinevere, without stopping to think if they were right or wrong."

Reading Notes

Castle of the Maiden	castle where the sick maiden lies
Enchanted Ship	ship that takes Dindrane and knights to Castle of the Maiden

Vocabulary

Write the meaning of each **bold** word or phrase.

1. I shall treat you as a **felon** and a traitor criminal, villain, lawbreaker
2. and **hew** you in pieces where you kneel to saw, cut
3. Cease this **strife**! conflict, contention, disagreement

Comprehension Questions

Answer the following in complete sentences.

1. How does Sir Bors learn that he will be successful in his quest? Naciens tells him that he will see the Grail.
2. What type of phantom tries to deceive Sir Bors? a lovely damsel
3. Why does Sir Bors' brother want to kill him? Sir Bors chooses to save an unknown woman over his own brother.
4. Who saves Sir Bors from his brother's rage? Naciens saves him.
5. What does Launcelot see when he rests by the altar and chapel? He sees the Grail descend on a moonbeam and heal a wounded knight.
6. Why does he not rise and grasp the Grail? He is held down by his sins.
7. What is his chief sin? He is in love with Guinevere.
8. What happens to Dindrane? She gives blood and heals the sick maiden. She bleeds to death and is placed upon the Enchanted Ship.

Discussion Questions

1. Who said the first quotation? Naciens To whom? Sir Bors
2. Who said the second quotation? Launcelot To whom? Naciens
3. How does the quest for the Holy Grail differ from the other quests in the book?
4. The code of chivalry placed emphasis on helping women in need. Does Sir Bors do the right thing by rescuing the woman rather than his brother? What are the consequences of his choice?

Enrichment

1. Write a paragraph comparing Naciens and Merlin. Are there any stories you know that have a character similar to Merlin? If so, include that in your paragraph.

"So shall the darkness fall upon Logres."

"And when he died this penance was laid on me:
that I should live beyond the span of mortal men to be the
Priest of the Grail until the coming of Sir Galahad the Good Knight."

Reading Notes

Grail Maiden Blanchefleur
Grail Priest Galahad

Vocabulary

Write the meaning of each **bold** word or phrase.

1. across the **bleak** uplands dreary, somber, depressing
2. Naciens … gave him **absolution** remission of sin, relief from guilt, forgiveness
3. said King Pelles in a **feeble** voice weak, frail
4. all his senses **forsook** him abandoned, deserted

Comprehension Questions

Answer the following in complete sentences.

1. Why does Gawain think he will not find the Holy Grail? He thinks he is unworthy.
2. What does this tell us about Gawain? He is humble.
3. What does Gawain see in the chapel after Sir Hector leaves? He sees a candlestick with seven candles and a black hand putting them out.
4. What does Gawain think this signifies? It signifies the darkness to fall on Logres.
5. How does Launcelot get a glimpse of the Holy Grail? He prays to be allowed to see something of what he seeks if he has ever pleased God.
6. Who is in the Chapel of the Holy Grail? The Grail Maiden (Blanchefleur) and Naciens are in the chapel.
7. How does Gawain take away the Curse of Desolation from Carbonek? He asks about the meaning of the procession.
8. Who leads the procession into the Chapel of the Holy Grail? Galahad

9. How does Galahad cure Pelles? Galahad uses the Holy Lance to drop blood onto Pelles' wound.

10. What happens to the Holy Grail after Galahad dies? It ascends into the heavens.

Discussion Questions

1. Read the first quotation. Who thought that? Gawain
2. What was he witnessing? a hand putting out candles
3. Who said the second quotation? Naciens To whom? Galahad
4. Half of the company in the Grail Chapel dies during the Grail ceremony. Is the outcome of the quest something to be celebrated or mourned? If the Grail were to appear again, do you think the knights would be so quick to chase after it?

Enrichment

1. Write a paragraph explaining which knights survived the quest and why.

2. Chivalry was like a list of rules which knights tried to obey at all times. Write down a list of ten rules which you try to obey every day.
   1) ______
   2) ______
   3) ______
   4) ______
   5) ______
   6) ______
   7) ______
   8) ______
   9) ______
   10) ______

"Come out and fight, and all your treacherous curs with you—
for here am I, Sir Launcelot of the Lake, ready to do battle with you all!"

Reading Notes

Melliagraunce	son of Bagdemagus
Mordred	the most evil knight in Logres

Vocabulary

Write the meaning of each **bold** word or phrase.

1. **dissension** to the whole realm of Logres strife, conflict, disagreement
2. Sir Melliagraunce **swaggered** about strutted
3. jealous of Sir Launcelot's fame and **renown** fame, celebrity

Comprehension Questions

Answer the following in complete sentences.

1. What happens when Guinevere goes riding in the woods with her friends? Melliagraunce, who loves Guinevere, surrounds her with his knights and kidnaps her.
2. What reminds King Arthur that Logres will soon fall? Launcelot heals Sir Urry. The Lady of the Lake had prophesied that when he healed someone again, Logres would soon pass.
3. What agreement do Launcelot and Melliagraunce come to when Guinevere is released from captivity? They agree to meet on a given date and fight each other.
4. How does Melliagraunce try to prevent the fight from taking place? He deceives Launcelot and traps him in a dungeon so that he will be unable to show up at the appointed time.
5. What does Mordred hear that pleases him so? He hears Guinevere and Launcelot profess their secret love and agreement to meet in secret.

Discussion Questions

1. Who said the quotation? Launcelot
2. Where was he? outside of Melliagraunce's castle
3. King Arthur remembers Nimue's prophecy of Logres' downfall. If you were in his position, how would you act when you knew that your kingdom was about to come to an end? Would you try to prevent it?
4. Merlin had prophesied that the end of Logres would be a result of Arthur's marriage to Guinevere. Why do you think King Arthur fails to pay special attention to Guinevere and how she spends her time?

Enrichment

1. The responses of Launcelot and Arthur to the news of Guinevere's kidnapping are markedly different. Compare the actions of Arthur and Launcelot in a paragraph.

"... here now you lie dying, the man whom I loved best in all the world. ... For you and Launcelot I loved best of all my knights: and I have lost you both."

Reading Notes

Colgrevaunce	knight involved in Mordred's conspiracy
Archbishop of Canterbury	high-ranking official of the church; this position was not created until 597 A.D.
Tower of London	place of imprisonment for British royalty; built by William the Conqueror

Vocabulary

Write the meaning of each **bold** word or phrase.

1. with lies and **slanders** in your mouths malicious falsehoods
2. Gawain **brooded** on his brothers' deaths worried, fretted, stewed
3. Gawain lying **mortally** wounded fatally (Latin: mors, mortis)

Comprehension Questions

Answer the following in complete sentences.

1. What is Arthur's reaction to the news of Guinevere's infidelity? He tells Mordred to gather twelve knights and kill Launcelot or take him prisoner.
2. Of what crime is Guinevere guilty? She is guilty of high treason.
3. What happens when Guinevere is led to the stake to be burnt? Launcelot arrives with his followers and rescues Guinevere.
4. Where does Launcelot go after returning Guinevere to King Arthur? He goes to France.
5. Why does Gawain become obsessed with killing Launcelot? Launcelot has killed Gawain's three brothers; he seeks revenge.
6. What happens in Logres while Arthur is in France fighting Launcelot? Mordred, whom Arthur leaves in charge, claims the throne. Guinevere flees to the Tower.
7. What is Gawain's last request? He asks for forgiveness, and he requests that Launcelot return to Logres to fight for Arthur.

Discussion Questions

1. Who said the quotation? Arthur To whom? Gawain
2. Arthur changes his mind twice in this chapter. He regrets his choice to burn Guinevere, and he asks Launcelot for peace after starting a fight with him. When Arthur once again pursues Launcelot in France, it is not his own choice, but he was "forced to declare war" on account of his knights' desires. What does this tell us about King Arthur's leadership skills? What does it tell us about the state of his power?
3. Launcelot offers to return Guinevere to Arthur and swear that she was innocent of any wrongdoing. Why would anyone believe Launcelot? Why does Arthur accept the offer?

Enrichment

1. "But some hours later Sir Gawain found King Arthur sitting all alone in the great empty hall in his place at the Round Table, with the tears running from his eyes and trickling unheeded through his grey beard and on to his hands." Write a paragraph explaining Arthur's feelings at this moment. Why do you think he is so quick to believe the worst of Guinevere and Launcelot? Why doesn't he seize on Gawain's excuse that there is no proof of wrongdoing? Write your answer in a paragraph.

"But be you sure that I will come again when the land of Britain has need of me, and the realm of Logres shall rise once more out of the darkness."

Reading Notes

Bedivere — the only surviving knight to keep the legend of Logres alive

Vocabulary

Write the meaning of each **bold** word or phrase.

1. **harrying** the lands ______ raiding, pillaging
2. for it is of no **avail**—and my time is short ______ help, benefit
3. the **meekest** and most gentle ______ most patient, humble, passive
4. The evening fell, dark and **ominous** ______ menacing, threatening

Comprehension Questions

Answer the following in complete sentences.

1. What does Gawain tell Arthur in the mysterious vision? ______ He advises him not to fight Mordred immediately but to wait one month for Launcelot to arrive.
2. How does the battle with Mordred begin? ______ Arthur is making peace with Mordred, but a soldier takes out his sword to kill a snake. Then both sides charge.
3. Why does Arthur attack Mordred? ______ He wants to punish Mordred for destroying Logres.
4. How does Arthur die? ______ He is struck on the head by Mordred.
5. What does Arthur ask Bedivere to do just before he dies? ______ He asks him three times to throw Excalibur into the lake.
6. Where is Arthur taken in the boat of women, and why is he taken there? ______ He is taken to the Vale of Avalon so that his head wound might heal.
7. What do Guinevere and Launcelot do to repent for their sins? ______ They each join a monastery.
8. Who controls Britain after Logres is destroyed? ______ the Saxons

9. What story is invented by the monks at Glastonbury, and why is it pleasing to the Norman rulers in Britain? The monks claim that they found a coffin with Arthur's bones inside. This pleases the Norman rulers because the Arthurian legend does not support Norman rule in Britain.

Discussion Questions

1. Who said the quotation? Arthur To whom? Sir Bedivere
2. Gawain speaks to Arthur in a vision. He says that he has been sent by God. He tells Arthur not to start battle with Mordred. Arthur obeys him, but due to the snake, battle commences anyway. Why didn't Gawain warn Arthur about such a possibility?
3. Sir Gawain tells Arthur that if he fights Mordred immediately, he will die. If he waits for Launcelot, he will be victorious. Arthur does fight Mordred, and the battle comes to an end with almost every warrior on the field dead or wounded. King Arthur and Mordred are both alive. Was Gawain's prediction false?
4. Sir Lucan advises Arthur to let Mordred leave the battleground unmolested. Had Arthur heeded this advice, it may be assumed that he would have lived. He did, however, attack Mordred. This brought Gawain's prophecy to fulfillment. Did Arthur have a choice in the matter?

Enrichment

1. On a separate sheet of paper, draw a line down the middle. At the top left write "History," and on the top right write "Fantasy." Write down which parts of the Arthurian legends you think may have been true on the left side of the line. Write down which parts are make-believe on the right side.
2. Read the excerpt from Tennyson's *Le Morte D'Arthur* in the Appendix. Rewrite Arthur's words in your own words.

Appendix

Glossary

A

absolution	*remission of sin; relief from guilt; forgiveness*
ancestry	*lineage*
anguish	*torment, distress, agonizing pain*
avail	*help, benefit*

B

bestow	*to confer, place*
bleak	*dreary, somber, depressing*
brooded	*worried, fretted, stewed*

C

churl	*a crude, ill-bred person*
clad	*clothed*
craven	*cowardly*

D

desolate	*deserted, isolated*
dire	*urgent; fearful*
dissension	*strife, conflict, disagreement*

F

feeble	*weak, frail*
felon	*criminal, villain, lawbreaker*
festered	*became infected, rotted, decayed*
forsook	*abandoned, deserted*
forthwith	*immediately*
fostered	*encouraged, nurtured, cared for*

G

Grail	*the cup of Jesus*

H

harrying	*raiding, pillaging*
hermit	*one who lives in solitude*
hew	*to saw, cut*
homage	*a ceremony by which a man acknowledged himself the vassal of a lord; special honor*

I

indistinct	*vague, hazy, murky*

L

lamentations	*expressions of grief; mournings*

M

meekest	*patient, humble, passive*
mockery	*ridicule, derision*
mortally	*fatally (Latin: mors, mortis)*

O

ominous	*menacing, threatening*

P

pavilion	*ornate tent*
peerless	*unequalled*
penance	*contrition, remorse, regret*
pensively	*thoughtfully, contemplatively*
perilous	*dangerous, risky*
plaintive	*sorrowful*
prospered	*succeeded*
prowess	*skill, aptitude*
purged	*purified, absolved, cleansed*

R

rash *reckless, careless*
rebuke *to reprove, criticize*
redeem *to pay off; to compensate for*
redress *amends*
renown *fame, celebrity*
restrain *to hold back*
reverence *awe; respect*

S

samite *silken cloth*
scornfully *contemptuously, disdainfully*
siege *seat, chair*
slanders *malicious falsehoods*
stead *place, position*
strife *conflict, contention, disagreement*
succour *to aid, assist, relieve*
swaggered *strutted*

T

taunted *ridiculed; provoked*
tremulous *trembling, quivering*

V

valiantly *bravely, courageously*
valour *heroism, courage*
vigil *a watch, surveillance*

W

wretched *miserable, woeful*

The Lady of Shalott

by Alfred Lord Tennyson

Part I

On either side the river lie
Long fields of barley and of rye,
That clothe the wold and meet the sky;
And through the field the road runs by
  To many-towered Camelot;
And up and down the people go,
Gazing where the lilies blow
Round an island there below,
  The island of Shalott.

Willows whiten, aspens quiver,
Little breezes dusk and shiver
Through the wave that runs for ever
By the island in the river
  Flowing down to Camelot.
Four grey walls, and four grey towers,
Overlook a space of flowers,
And the silent isle imbowers
  The Lady of Shalott.

By the margin, willow-veiled,
Slide the heavy barges trailed
By slow horses; and unhailed
The shallop flitteth silken-sailed
  Skimming down to Camelot:
But who hath seen her wave her hand?
Or at the casement seen her stand?
Or is she known in all the land,
  The Lady of Shalott?

Only reapers, reaping early
In among the bearded barley,
Hear a song that echoes cheerly
From the river winding clearly,
  Down to towered Camelot:
And by the moon the reaper weary,
Piling sheaves in uplands airy,
Listening, whispers "'Tis the fairy
  Lady of Shalott."

Part II

There she weaves by night and day
A magic web with colours gay.
She has heard a whisper say,
A curse is on her if she stay
  To look down to Camelot.
She knows not what the curse may be,
And so she weaveth steadily,
And little other care hath she,
  The Lady of Shalott.

And moving through a mirror clear
That hangs before her all the year,
Shadows of the world appear.
There she sees the highway near
  Winding down to Camelot:
There the river eddy whirls,
And there the surly village-churls,
And the red cloaks of market girls,
  Pass onward from Shalott.

Sometimes a troop of damsels glad,
An abbot on an ambling pad,
Sometimes a curly shepherd-lad,
Or long-haired page in crimson clad,
  Goes by to towered Camelot;
And sometimes through the mirror blue
The knights come riding two and two:
She hath no loyal knight and true,
  The Lady of Shalott.

But in her web she still delights
To weave the mirror's magic sights,
For often through the silent nights
A funeral, with plumes and lights
  And music, went to Camelot:
Or when the moon was overhead,
Came two young lovers lately wed;
"I am half sick of shadows," said
  The Lady of Shalott.

Part III

A bow-shot from her bower-eaves,
He rode between the barley-sheaves,
The sun came dazzling through the leaves,
And flamed upon the brazen greaves
  Of bold Sir Lancelot.
A red-cross knight for ever kneeled
To a lady in his shield,
That sparkled on the yellow field,
  Beside remote Shalott.

The gemmy bridle glittered free,
Like to some branch of stars we see
Hung in the golden Galaxy.
The bridle bells rang merrily
  As he rode down to Camelot:
And from his blazoned baldric slung
A mighty silver bugle hung,
And as he rode his armour rung,
  Beside remote Shalott.

All in the blue unclouded weather
Thick-jewelled shone the saddle-leather,
The helmet and the helmet-feather
Burned like one burning flame together,
  As he rode down to Camelot.
As often through the purple night,
Below the starry clusters bright,
Some bearded meteor, trailing light,
  Moves over still Shalott.

His broad clear brow in sunlight glowed;
On burnished hooves his war-horse trode;
From underneath his helmet flowed
His coal-black curls as on he rode,
  As he rode down to Camelot.
From the bank and from the river
He flashed into the crystal mirror,
"Tirra lirra," by the river
  Sang Sir Lancelot.

She left the web, she left the loom,
She made three paces through the room,
She saw the water-lily bloom,
She saw the helmet and the plume,
  She looked down to Camelot.
Out flew the web and floated wide;
The mirror cracked from side to side;
"The curse is come upon me," cried
  The Lady of Shalott.

Part IV

In the stormy east-wind straining,
The pale yellow woods were waning,
The broad stream in his banks complaining,
Heavily the low sky raining
  Over towered Camelot;
Down she came and found a boat
Beneath a willow left afloat,
And round about the prow she wrote
  The Lady of Shalott.

And down the river's dim expanse,
Like some bold seer in a trance
Seeing all his own mischance—
With a glassy countenance
  Did she look to Camelot.
And at the closing of the day
She loosed the chain, and down she lay;
The broad stream bore her far away,
  The Lady of Shalott.

Lying, robed in snowy white
That loosely flew to left and right—
The leaves upon her falling light—
Through the noises of the night
  She floated down to Camelot:
And as the boat-head wound along
The willowy hills and fields among,
They heard her singing her last song,
  The Lady of Shalott.

Heard a carol, mournful, holy,
Chanted loudly, chanted lowly,
Till her blood was frozen slowly,
And her eyes were darkened wholly,
  Turned to towered Camelot.
For ere she reached upon the tide
The first house by the water-side,
Singing in her song she died,
  The Lady of Shalott.

Under tower and balcony,
By garden-wall and gallery,
A gleaming shape she floated by,
Dead-pale between the houses high,
  Silent into Camelot.

Out upon the wharfs they came,
Knight and burgher, lord and dame,
And round the prow they read her name,
  The Lady of Shalott.

Who is this? and what is here?
And in the lighted palace near
Died the sound of royal cheer;
And they crossed themselves for fear,
  All the knights at Camelot:
But Lancelot mused a little space;
He said, "She has a lovely face;
God in his mercy lend her grace,
  The Lady of Shalott."

The Wooing of Sir Keith

by Howard Pyle

King Arthur sat in his royal hall,
  And about on either hand
Was many a noble lordling tall,
  The greatest in the land.

Sat Lancelot with raven locks,
  Gawaine with golden hair,
Sir Tristram, Kay who kept the locks,
  And many another there.

And through the stained windows bright,
  From o'er the red-tiled eaves,
The sunlight blazed with colored light
  On golden helms and greaves.

But suddenly a silence came
  About the Table Round,
For up the hall there walked a dame
  Bent nigh unto the ground.

Her nose was hooked, her eyes were bleared,
  Her locks were lank and white;
Upon her chin there grew a beard;
  She was a gruesome sight.

And so with crawling step she came
  And kneeled at Arthur's feet;
Quoth Kay, 'She is the foulest dame
  That e'er my sight did greet.'

'O mighty King! of thee I crave
  A boon on bended knee';
'Twas thus she spoke. 'What wouldst thou have.'
  Quoth Arthur, King, 'of me?'

Quoth she, 'I have a foul disease
  Doth gnaw my very heart,
And but one thing can bring me ease
  Or cure my bitter smart.

'There is no rest, no ease for me
  North, east, or west, or south,
Till Christian knight will willingly
  Thrice kiss me on the mouth.

'Nor wedded may this childe have been
  That giveth ease to me;
Nor may he be constrained, I ween,
  But kiss me willingly.

'So is there here one Christian knight
  Of such a noble strain
That he will give a tortured wight
  Sweet ease of mortal pain?'

'A wedded man,' quoth Arthur, King,
  'A wedded man I be
Else would I deem it noble thing
  To kiss thee willingly.

'Now, Lancelot, in all men's sight
  Thou art the head and chief
Of chivalry. Come, noble knight,
  And give her quick relief.'

But Lancelot he turned aside
  And looked upon the ground,
For it did sting his haughty pride
  To hear them laugh around.

'Come thou, Sir Tristram,' quoth the King.
  Quoth he, 'It cannot be,
For ne'er can I my stomach bring
  To do it willingly.'

'Wilt thou, Sir Kay, thou scornful wight?'
  Quoth Kay, 'Nay, by my troth!
What noble dame would kiss a knight
  That kissed so foul a mouth?'

'Wilt thou, Gawaine?' 'I cannot, King.'
  'Sir Geraint?' 'Nay, not I;

My kisses no relief could bring,
  For sooner would I die.'

Then up and spake the youngest man
  Of all about the board,
'Now such relief as Christian can
  I'll give to her, my lord.'

It was Sir Keith, a youthful knight,
  Yet strong of limb and bold,
With beard upon his chin as light
  As finest threads of gold.

Quoth Kay, 'He hath no mistress yet
  That he may call his own,
But here is one that's quick to get,
  As she herself has shown.'

He kissed her once, he kissed her twice,
  He kissed her three times o'er,
A wondrous change came in a trice,
  And she was foul no more.

Her cheeks grew red as any rose,
  Her brow as white as lawn,
Her bosom like the winter snows,
  Her eyes like those of fawn.

Her breath grew sweet as summer breeze
  That blows the meadows o'er;
Her voice grew soft as rustling trees,
  And cracked and harsh no more.

Her hair grew glittering, like the gold,
  Her hands as white as milk;
Her filthy rags, so foul and old,
  Were changed to robes of silk.

In great amaze the knights did stare.
  Quoth Kay, 'I make my vow
If it will please thee, lady fair,
  I'll gladly kiss thee now.'

But young Sir Keith kneeled on one knee
  And kissed her robes so fair.
'O let me be thy slave,' said he,
  'For none to thee compare.'

She bent her down, she kissed his brow,
  She kissed his lips and eyes.
Quoth she, 'Thou art my master now,
  My lord, my love, arise!

'And all the wealth that is mine own,
  My lands, I give to thee,
For never knight hath lady shown
  Such noble courtesy.

'Bewitched was I, in bitter pain,
  But thou hast set me free,
So now I am myself again,
  I give myself to thee.'

from Le Morte D'Arthur

by Alfred Lord Tennyson

Then loudly cried the bold Sir Bedivere,
"Ah! my Lord Arthur, whither shall I go?
Where shall I hide my forehead and my eyes?
For now I see the true old times are dead,
When every morning brought a noble chance,
And every chance brought out a noble knight.
Such times have been not since the light that led
The holy Elders with the gift of myrrh.
But now the whole ROUND TABLE is dissolved
Which was an image of the mighty world;
And I, the last, go forth companionless,
And the days darken round me, and the years,
Among new men, strange faces, other minds."

And slowly answered Arthur from the barge:
"The old order changeth, yielding place to new,
And God fulfils Himself in many ways,
Lest one good custom should corrupt the world.
Comfort thyself: what comfort is in me?
I have lived my life, and that which I have done
May He within Himself make pure! but thou,
If thou shouldst never see my face again,
Pray for my soul. More things are wrought by prayer
Than this world dreams of. Wherefore, let thy voice
Rise like a fountain for me night and day.
For what are men better than sheep or goats
That nourish a blind life within the brain,
If, knowing God, they lift not hands of prayer
Both for themselves and those who call them friend?
For so the whole round earth is every way
Bound by gold chains about the feet of God.
But now farewell. I am going a long way
With these thou seest—if indeed I go—
(For all my mind is clouded with a doubt)
To the island-valley of Avilion;
Where falls not hail, or rain, or any snow,
Nor ever wind blows loudly; but it lies
Deep-meadowed, happy, fair with orchard-lawns
And bowery hollows crowned with summer sea,
Where I will heal me of my grievous wound."

So said he, and the barge with oar and sail
Moved from the brink, like some full-breasted swan
That, fluting a wild carol ere her death,
Ruffles her pure cold plume, and takes the flood
With swarthy webs. Long stood Sir Bedivere
Revolving many memories, till the hull
Looked one black dot against the verge of dawn,
And on the mere the wailing died away.

Discussion Questions
Answer Key

Book 1, Chapter 1

Look at the picture on the page preceding Chapter 1 in your book. Who is in the picture? What castle is in the background? What is happening?

In the picture Merlin is fleeing Tintagel with the baby Arthur. He did this because he could see how important Arthur would be for Britain's future.

If you had to divide this chapter into two different parts, where would you divide it, and why?

The chapter divides nicely into two sections. Pages 3-13 are introductory. This first half of the chapter explains who Arthur is and how he became King of Britain. Near the middle of the chapter, the narrative shifts to the first "adventure" of the book. The rest of the chapter tells the story of King Pellinore and how Arthur acquired Excalibur.

Book 1, Chapter 2

The Lady of the Lake is killed in Arthur's court. Arthur neither honors her request nor protects her from Balyn. Does this reveal a weakness in Arthur?

King Arthur's refusal to honor his promise to the Lady of the Lake makes a mockery of the code of chivalry which he lays forth in Chapter 1. For a murder to occur in the very presence of the king reveals great irresponsibility on the part of Arthur. Granted, Balyn may have made a swift move when he attacked the Lady of the Lake, but such an honored guest should have been brought near the king with an armed guard.

Who was Joseph of Arimathea? Is it possible that he took the Grail to Britain?

The Gospels tell us that Joseph of Arimathea was a Jewish counselor and a secret follower of Jesus. After the Crucifixion, Joseph asked Pilate for Jesus' body so that he could bury him in a tomb. The story of Joseph's trip to England is largely based on the text of a 12th-century French poet, Robert de Boron.

Book 1, Chapter 3

The feasts at Camelot are held on Christian holidays such as Pentecost and Easter. Does this give us insight into the type of kingdom over which Arthur was ruling?

Christianity had reached England, according to the Venerable Bead, around the year 1. The religion was adopted and became part of a Romano-British culture. It was this culture which King Arthur was promoting and preserving. The "heathen Saxons" were a threat to Christianity. One of his first orders of business upon becoming king was to "rebuild the churches which they have destroyed, and build new ones to the glory of God" (p. 13).

Why do you think Arthur chooses to marry Guinevere even after Merlin tells him that she will bring an end to Logres?

Perhaps it is due to the fact that prophecies are about things that can't be seen, but Guinevere's beauty is quite visible to Arthur. He can see the benefit of marrying Guinevere, but it takes faith to act in accordance with Merlin's advice.

Book 1, Chapter 4

This is not the first time that two knights have mistakenly fought to the death. It seems that if two knights lack their own shields and have visors down, then they are at risk of killing even a family member. Can you think of a way that such tragedies could have been avoided?

It may have been useful to have a formal introduction between the two knights that were about to fight. Because honor was so highly esteemed, it is possible that such men could agree to reveal their identities with honesty. Perhaps there could have been a third party that stood between the warriors before the fight and asked each person his name. The third party could then keep the identities secret if the fighters were not friends or relatives, but he could cancel the battle if they would later regret their fight.

Why do you think Arthur would rather "die a hundred times" than to admit that he was beaten and cowardly?

It is hard for us to imagine someone accepting death by a sword wound rather than admitting cowardice. Chivalry, however, was taken so seriously that shame and honor were considered more important than life or death (or pleasure or pain). The ideals of chivalry gave life meaning, and if a knight were to forsake those ideals, he may lose his desire to live.

Book 2, Chapter 1

In the legends, many battles took place in which a knight refused to submit to his opponent even though he was defeated. Such knights appear to have valued their honor more than life itself. Gawain acted differently. Though he did not yield to the Green Knight, he kept a secret lace which protected him from harm. Do you think his behavior was honorable?

Gawain's behavior was a consequence of his love for life. Sir Bernlak said that such a trait was a small sin. It does seem natural to prefer life over death, especially when one is about to offer their neck to the edge of an axe.

Gawain's discreet possession of a magic lace is similar to King Arthur's scabbard. Each item protected its bearer from being killed. The chivalric code placed upon all knights the requirement of being honest at all times. Neither Gawain nor Arthur told their opponents of their secret protection. Is this honest? Does it conflict with the chivalric code?

It could be considered contradictory for knights to promise to be honest and then conceal the possession of a magical item which protects them. Even though the item is not a danger to their enemy, the opposing knights surely would prefer to know if it were possible for them to win a fight against Arthur or Gawain. So long as Arthur carried the scabbard, he was nearly invincible. His refusal to reveal his protection to his enemies shows that Arthur did not respect them. The result was a fight that was not fair. A chivalric knight would not take part in an unfair fight.

Book 2, Chapter 2

How can a knight heal someone by simply touching the person? Does this mean that knights have special powers?

There is magic involved in almost all of these stories. Being able to heal someone by touch is simply a way of showing how Launcelot is a special character in the story. There is no hint in the book that this magic is controlled or controllable. The magic serves as a storytelling device.

Many prophesies were made regarding the pending destruction of Logres. Why did Arthur and his knights fail to discuss how they could preserve Logres? What type of strategy might they have devised?

Establishing Logres would have consumed much of Arthur's time. Perhaps it was immediately after gaining power that the quests began. If that were the case, it may have been simply a problem of time management. The knights may have had difficulty synchronizing their schedules for a mass meeting.

Book 2, Chapter 3

Why do you think Sir Gareth puts up with Lady Linnet for so long? Do you think Sir Gareth behaves honorably to Lady Linnet? Would you have done likewise?

Beaumains is probably acting in full accord with the code of chivalry. Honoring women and treating them with respect apparently had no limits.

Is there a lesson to be learned in this story? What do you think it is?

Among the multiple lessons that might be gathered from this story is the following: Patience and tolerance sometimes lead to a great reward.

Book 2, Chapter 4

Siege Perilous, along with the neighboring chairs, is reserved for very brave knights. Does this hierarchy of seats defeat the purpose of the round table?

Having privileged seats at the Round Table makes it just like a rectangular table. The original problem was that knights were arguing about who would sit closest to the king. Now the knights have reason to want to sit closest to Perilous. The Round Table, however, has names at each seat. The magical nature of the table may keep the knights from trying to sit at a seat with someone else's name on it.

This legend was influenced by other famous stories and myths. Did any part of this story remind you of another story you've heard?

When the merchants think that the storm is due to Tristram's presence on the ship, they get him off of their boat. The story of Jonah is similar. When Marhault demands the yearly tribute of thirty young nobles, Tristram brings an end to the shameful payments. The story of Theseus is similar. The mention of black and white sails leading to someone's death is also similar to the story of Theseus.

Book 2, Chapter 6

Why do you think Morgana le Fay keeps trying to kill Arthur?

Perhaps she is jealous. Perhaps she is a bad witch by nature.

Book 2, Chapter 7

Do you find it hard to believe that a boy who grew up in the woods could defeat a trained knight with a dart?

It does seem unlikely that anyone could defeat a knight in full armor that has not been especially trained to do so. However, Percivale may have learned to be sneaky and quick while growing up in the woods.

Does Percivale's defeat of the knight in golden-red armor remind you of a Bible story?

The story of David killing Goliath with a stone bears similarity to this story.

Book 2, Chapter 8

After professing his love to the wrong woman, Launcelot goes mad because he feels dishonored. What do you think honor means? Why do you think it was so important to knights? Is it important to people today?

> Honor can be considered a reward, or the quality of having a good name. It remains important to people today. However, the importance of honor in our lives today is hardly comparable to the role it played in the life of a chivalrous medieval knight.

Book 3, Chapter 1

Upon taking the sword from the stone, Galahad declares, "Now I have the sword that struck the Dolorous Stroke." Is this true? Why does he say this?

> The "Dolorous Stroke" was not made with a sword. Therefore, the sword in question is not the sword that struck the Dolorous Stroke. Why Galahad would say such a thing is a mystery. The famous stroke was made with a lance. The sword would be more correctly referred to as "the sword that belonged to the man (Balyn) that struck the Dolorous Stroke using a lance."

The vision of the Holy Grail shared among all the knights is described as filling each man with the joy and peace of God. The knights consider the vision unsatisfactory and vow to not only view the Grail, but to touch it as well. Why do you think they take the vision as a challenge to find the Grail?

> If the context of the vision is considered, then it is not surprising that the knights would chase after the Grail. It was custom that feasts would not begin before a quest was introduced to the knights. Such quests were usually presented in the hall of the Round Table in some strange manner. The vision of the Grail took place at the time and space that all quests began, at the table before a feast. Therefore, they interpreted it as a quest to be followed rather than a blessing to be enjoyed and reflected upon.

Why do you think the knights pursue the Grail in groups of twos and threes rather than staying together?

> It may be that the legends were stories about single knights, or knights in pairs. If the knights were to travel and act as a group, it would have been more difficult for minstrels to distinguish individuals as paragons of virtue. But if each legend focused on one knight, the minstrels could weave a cohesive lay which focused on a single hero.

Book 3, Chapters 2 and 3

Why do you think Sir Galahad chooses to take the easy path rather than the challenging path? Is there honor in that?

> Perhaps Galahad is so focused on finding the Grail that he doesn't care about honor gained in other pursuits. The only goal he is concerned about is the honor gained by attaining the Holy Grail.

The lady who tempts Percivale to betray his oath made to Blanchefleur is obviously trying to ruin his quest. The black horse, however, seems to help Percivale in his quest. Why do you think the horse, which is a demon, helps Percivale?

> Percivale thinks that the horse is going to carry him to hell. But at no time does the horse take Percivale anywhere but in the direction Percivale desires. Maybe the horse is running towards an evil stable to eat oats before the long trip to hell.

Book 3, Chapters 4 and 5

How does the quest for the Holy Grail differ from the other quests in the book?

This quest demands that a knight possess virtues. Humility and purity are required of knights. It is for this reason that Launcelot, the knight who exceeds all others in valor and fighting skills, is denied the privilege of touching the Grail.

The code of chivalry placed emphasis on helping women in need. Does Sir Bors do the right thing by rescuing the woman rather than his brother? What are the consequences of his choice?

Sir Bors does act in obedience to the code as presented by Arthur. In that code, knights are commanded to help those in need. Both his brother and the lady are in need. The code goes on to mention women as requiring the knights' utmost efforts. It makes no mention of family members. The consequences are mixed. He wastes his time trying to rescue a woman who turns out to be an evil spirit. At the same time, he resists temptation and thereby becomes worthy of seeing the Grail. His brother kills a monk in his anger and then spends a year doing penance.

Book 3, Chapters 6 and 7

Half of the company in the Grail Chapel dies during the Grail ceremony. Is the outcome of the quest something to be celebrated or mourned? If the Grail were to appear again, do you think the knights would be so quick to chase after it?

The deaths might be viewed as blessings. It might be assumed that each person who died went straight to heaven. If that was the chief desire of the deceased, then completion of the quest was a blessing to everyone. However, it is not clear that Sir Galahad desired to die rather than continue serving King Arthur. It is possible that some knights of the Round Table would prefer to live a long life gaining glory and honor in their adventures rather than passively die after touching the Grail. If the Grail were to come again into the court of King Arthur, there may be some knights who would politely decline the quest.

Book 4, Chapter 1

King Arthur remembers Nimue's prophecy of Logres' downfall. If you were in his position, how would you act when you knew that your kingdom was about to come to an end? Would you try to prevent it?

Even if your kingdom's downfall seemed inevitable, if you were living by the code of chivalry, you would do whatever possible to prevent it, for as long as possible.

Merlin had prophesied that the end of Logres would be a result of Arthur's marriage to Guinevere. Why do you think King Arthur fails to pay special attention to Guinevere and how she spends her time?

King Arthur fails to take precautions against Guinevere's infidelity for the same reason that he marries her in the first place; because when he is around her he stops thinking logically.

Book 4, Chapter 2

Arthur changes his mind twice in this chapter. He regrets his choice to burn Guinevere, and he asks Launcelot for peace after starting a fight with him. When Arthur once again pursues Launcelot in France, it is not his own choice, but he "was forced to declare war" on account of his knights' desires. What does this tell us about King Arthur's leadership skills? What does it tell us about the state of his power?

These are not traits of a decisive and able ruler. Perhaps Arthur is getting old. It is not a sign of power when a king is forced to go to war because his nobles desire it.

Launcelot offers to return Guinevere to Arthur and swear that she was innocent of any wrongdoing. Why would anyone believe Launcelot? Why does Arthur accept the offer?

Launcelot and King Arthur would have needed to put a positive spin on the entire story to prevent a scandal. It is possible it would have been believed, but the rumors and the truth would likely have spread among his knights. Arthur accepts the offer because he has become a weak king and desires to preserve the status quo above anything else.

Book 4, Chapter 3 and Epilogue

Gawain speaks to Arthur in a vision. He says that he has been sent by God. He tells Arthur not to start battle with Mordred. Arthur obeys him, but due to the snake, battle commences anyway. Why didn't Gawain warn Arthur about such a possibility?

Maybe God sent Gawain but did not tell him exactly what to say.

Sir Gawain tells Arthur that if he fights Mordred immediately, he will die. If he waits for Launcelot, he will be victorious. Arthur does fight Mordred, and the battle comes to an end with almost every warrior on the field dead or wounded. King Arthur and Mordred are both alive. Was Gawain's prediction false?

At that point in time, the prediction was false. Moments later, after Arthur made the choice to run at Mordred, the prophecy became true.

Sir Lucan advises Arthur to let Mordred leave the battleground unmolested. Had Arthur heeded this advice, it may be assumed that he would have lived. He did, however, attack Mordred. This brought Gawain's prophecy to fulfillment. Did Arthur have a choice in the matter?

Yes—He had fought with Mordred and survived, proving that Gawain's prophecy was false. The prophecy, therefore, did not hold sway over events, and he had free will.

No—The prophecy spanned the entire day, not just the climax of the battle. It also took into account the moment after the fighting had finished and Arthur chose to run after Mordred. He did not have a choice because the prophecy would be fulfilled no matter what.

Quizzes & Final Exam

(reproducible for classroom use)

King Arthur: Book I Quiz

Name:____________________ Date: ____________ Score: ________
64 total pts.

FACTS TO KNOW: Match each word below with the correct description. (1 pt. each)

Avalon	Castle Carbonek	Holy Grail	King Pellinore	Saxons
Balan	Excaliber	Igrayne	King Ryon	Sir Accolon
Balyn	Garlon	King Pant & Elayne	King Urience	Sir Uwaine
Camelot	Gawain	King Pelles	Logres	Uther Pendragon

1. ____________________ place where the Holy Grail resides; place of the Dolorous Stroke

2. ____________________ has the quest of the Questing Beast

3. ____________________ king and queen of North Wales; parents of Launcelot

4. ____________________ the invisible knight

5. ____________________ brother of Balyn; the one Balyn loved most in the world

6. ____________________ Germanic tribe that invaded Britain in the 5th & 6th centuries

7. ____________________ name of Arthur's kingdom

8. ____________________ cruel king of North Wales

9. ____________________ husband of Morgana

10. ____________________ capital of Arthur's kingdom; modern-day Winchester, England

11. ____________________ the cup Jesus drank from at the Last Supper

12. ____________________ son of Morgana and Urience

13. ____________________ the sword of Arthur

14. ____________________ king of Briton; father of Arthur

15. ____________________ king of Castle Carbonek; victim of the Dolorous Stroke

16. ____________________ son of Lot and Morgawse; nephew of Arthur

17. ____________________ knight who struck the Dolorous Stroke

18. ____________________ Land of Mystery; place where Merlin took Arthur as an infant

19. ____________________ Arthur's knight who loves Morgana le Fay

20. ____________________ wife of Gorlois, then Uther; mother of Arthur, Morgawse, Elaine, & Margana

VOCABULARY: Write the correct vocabulary word in the blanks below. (1 pt. each)

1. Set a rich ______________________ (ornate tent) over the stone.
2. Merlin told the knights to go out to ______________________ (aid, assist) gentlewomen.
3. You may______________________ (retrieve) your honor by some brave deed.
4. Sir Ector bowed his head in ______________________ (awe, respect) before Arthur.
5. "I am going to hit you again!" ______________________ (jeered, ridiculed) Sir Accolon.
6. The damsel made many ______________________ (expressions of grief) in her sorrow.
7. Yield you to me as ______________________ (cowardly) and vanquished.
8. The knights did ______________________ (special honor) to Arthur, swearing to serve and obey him.
9. We lay this ______________________ (contrition, remorse) upon you, that you bear the body.
10. Upon every ______________ (seat, chair) at the table was the name of the knight in letters of gold.

MULTIPLE CHOICE (1 pt. each)

1. King Arthur's foster father:
   - **a.** Sir Ector
   - **b.** Sir Gawain
   - **c.** Uther
2. Balyn kills the Lady of the Lake by:
   - **a.** beheading her
   - **b.** stabbing her heart
   - **c.** shooting her with an arrow
3. Arthur has to fight a war against:
   - **a.** 10 kings
   - **b.** 12 kings
   - **c.** 15 kings
4. Balan does not recognize Balyn because he does not have his own:
   - **a.** shield
   - **b.** sword
   - **c.** armor
5. Merlin says the person who will bring about the downfall of Logres is:
   - **a.** Launcelot
   - **b.** Guinevere
   - **c.** Morgana
6. The knight whose coming to the Round Table signifies one year before the Holy Grail comes:
   - **a.** Gawain
   - **b.** Launcelot
   - **c.** Percivale
7. The best knight of all will sit in the:
   - **a.** Siege Perilous
   - **b.** Siege Dangerous
   - **c.** Siege Sinister
8. Gawain learns from his quest to:
   - **a.** always be merciful
   - **b.** joust
   - **c.** never ignore a cry for help
9. Who buries Merlin while he is still alive?
   - **a.** Morgana
   - **b.** Lady Nimue
   - **c.** Elayne
10. Where was Arthur when he woke from his deep sleep upon the boat?
    - **a.** Camelot
    - **b.** beside a deep well
    - **c.** Sir Damas' castle

QUOTATIONS (2 pts. each)

1. "A little while after his birth at dark Tintagel, Uther, who hearkened to my words, gave the child into my care, and I bore him to Avalon, the Land of Mystery."

   Who said it?____________________ To whom? ____________________

2. "Bury us, I pray you, in the same tomb, and write upon it that here lie two brothers who slew one another by mischance ..."

   Who said it?____________________ To whom? ____________________

3. "Yet I would that you loved another; for by her very beauty shall come the end of Logres."

   Who said it?____________________ To whom? ____________________

4. "A knight without mercy is dishonoured: but to kill a fair lady is shame unto the world's end!"

   Who said it?____________________ To whom? ____________________

5. "For though I lack a weapon, yet shall I lack no honour—and if you slay me weaponless, it is you who will be shamed."

   Who said it?____________________ To whom? ____________________

6. "I have loved her long, and she me. And I promised to fight and slay whom she would, even though it were Arthur the King."

   Who said it?____________________ To whom? ____________________

COMPREHENSION QUESTIONS (3 pts. each)

1. What is Arthur's first goal as king?

   ____

   ____

2. Why is it called the "Dolorous Stroke" when Balyn strikes Pelles?

   ____

   ____

3. What is the purpose of the round table?

   ____

   ____

4. What happens to Excalibur's scabbard?

   ____

   ____

King Arthur: Book II, Chapters 1-4 Quiz

Name:______________________________ Date: ______________ Score: ________

60 total pts.

FACTS TO KNOW: Match each word below with the correct description. (1 pt. each)

Allewes	King Mark	Lionel	Sir Bernlak
Castle Dangerous	King Rivalin	Mordred	Sir Gareth
Hector	Lady Linnet	Morgan the Wicked	Sir Ironside
King Gurman	Lady Liones	Rual	Tintagel

1. ____________________ brother of Gawain, Gaheris, and Agravaine; Knight of the Kitchen
2. ____________________ son of Morgana le Fay; Arthur's nephew
3. ____________________ killer of Rivalin and usurper of his throne
4. ____________________ name of castle the Red Knight is besieging; home of Lady Liones
5. ____________________ King Mark's castle in Cornwall; castle where Igrayne was tricked by Uther
6. ____________________ Launcelot's cousin
7. ____________________ Launcelot's half-brother
8. ____________________ father of Tristram; king of Lyonesse
9. ____________________ Knight of the Lake; the Green Knight
10. ____________________ Red Knight; under the spell of Morgana le Fay
11. ____________________ king of Ireland; father of Iseult
12. ____________________ evil sorceress; companion of Morgana le Fay
13. ____________________ king of Cornwall; Tristram's uncle
14. ____________________ sister of Lady Linnet; practices evil magic
15. ____________________ servant of Rivalin who raises Tristram
16. ____________________ damsel in distress; needs aid of Arthur's knights

VOCABULARY: Write the correct vocabulary word in the blanks below. (1 pt. each)

1. I am no scullion, and of nobler ______________________________ (lineage) than you are!
2. The green knight cast some ______________________ (fearful, ominous) enchantment upon everyone.
3. ________________________________ (to confer, place) upon him the high order of knighthood.
4. It's only a _________________________ (miserable, woeful) kitchen knave.
5. They could not _____________________ (hold back) the tears from running down their cheeks.
6. Tristram's wound ___________________ (became infected, rotted, decayed) and might not be cured.
7. Lady Linnet laughed aloud in _______________________________ (ridicule, derision) at Gareth.
8. The child was lovingly __________________________ (encouraged, nurtured, cared for) by his parents.
9. You are uncourteous so to _____________________ (reprove, criticize) me and mock at me.
10. Launcelot was the _____________________________ (unequalled) knight of whom Merlin had spoken.

MULTIPLE CHOICE (1 pt. each)

1. The Green Knight has come to Arthur's court to test the Round Table's:
   - **a.** strength
   - **b.** skill
   - **c.** bravery
2. Gawain is to look for the Green Knight in:
   - **a.** 1 month
   - **b.** 1 year + 1 day
   - **c.** 6 months + 1 day
3. The person who sent the Green Knight to Arthur's court was:
   - **a.** Merlin
   - **b.** Morgana
   - **c.** Nimue
4. Launcelot chooses a dungeon over:
   - **a.** death by sword
   - **b.** four beautiful women
   - **c.** thirty black knights
5. Morgana's servant cries when releasing Launcelot because she:
   - **a.** loves him
   - **b.** is afraid he will die
   - **c.** hates him
6. The chapel where Launcelot has to go to save the injured knight is the Chapel___________.
   - **a.** Perilous
   - **b.** Dangerous
   - **c.** Dolorous
7. The third gift the Knight of the Kitchen requests is to be knighted by:
   - **a.** Gawain
   - **b.** Arthur
   - **c.** Launcelot
8. The Knight of the Kitchen gets his sword from:
   - **a.** Launcelot
   - **b.** a dwarf
   - **c.** Gawain
9. Sir Gareth's brother is:
   - **a.** Gawain
   - **b.** Launcelot
   - **c.** The Red Knight
10. Lady Liones marries:
    - **a.** Gareth
    - **b.** Gaheris
    - **c.** Gawain

11. The best knight Launcelot has ever jousted with is:
    - a. Gawain
    - b. Percivale
    - c. Tristram

12. To save thirty lads of Cornwall, Tristram fights and kills:
    - a. Morgan
    - b. Marhault
    - c. Mordred

13. To avenge the death of her brother, Queen Isaud keeps:
    - a. A dragon's tooth
    - b. A piece of a shirt
    - c. A sword chip

14. When Mark finds out Tristram and Iseult love each other, Tristram is:
    - a. Beheaded
    - b. Put in prison
    - c. Banished

QUOTATIONS (2 pts. each)

1. "As for the lace, you hid it but for love of your life—and that is a little sin, and for it I pardon you."

   Who said it?____________________ To whom? ____________________

2. "Merlin has spoken his name to you—and see, that name grows in letters of gold upon the empty siege on the right hand of the Siege Perilous!"

   Who said it?____________________ To whom? ____________________

3. "When you are a noble knight of noble birth, you shall have my love—but not before!"

   Who said it?____________________ To whom? ____________________

4. "Only Launcelot bowed his head in his hands, and the tears ran between his fingers as he thought of his own love for Guinevere."

   Why does Launcelot cry? ____

COMPREHENSION QUESTIONS (3 pts. each)

1. What is the challenge posed by the Green Knight, and who accepts it?

   ____

   ____

   ____

2. Launcelot faces three perils at the Chapel Perilous before he can come safely away with the sword and cloth. Name the three perils.

   ____

   ____

   ____

3. Why does Lady Linnet begin to think Gareth may be of noble birth?

____

____

____

4. How does Iseult discover Tristram's true identity?

____

____

____

King Arthur: Book II, Chapters 5-8 Quiz

Name:_______________ Date: _______________ Score: _______________

57 total pts.

FACTS TO KNOW: Match each word below with the correct description. (1 pt. each)

Blanchefleur	Duke Liconal	Elaine of Astolat	Lady Ragnell	Sir Oringle
Dolorous Lady	Duke Yder	Gromer Somer Joure	Sir Gonemans	

1. _______________ the giant knight who struck fear into anyone who approached
2. _______________ evil knight who struck Enid in the face
3. _______________ Percivale's love
4. _______________ imprisoned in scalding water by Morgana le Fay
5. _______________ Percivale's tutor in the art of knighthood
6. _______________ under the curse of Morgana; marries Gawain
7. _______________ knight who withheld nephew's inheritance from him
8. _______________ daughter of King Pelles; in love with Launcelot
9. _______________ rightful heir of Duke Liconal's dukedom

VOCABULARY: Write the correct vocabulary word in the blanks below. (1 pt. each)

1. A vile _______________ (crude, ill-bred person) this dwarf is!
2. He turned away with a cry of _______________ (torment, distress).
3. A damsel lay sleeping on a couch of rich silk and _______________ (silken cloth).
4. Elaine _______________ (succeeded) not at all in her love.
5. Percivale looked _______________ (disdainfully, contemptuously) at Sir Kay.
6. Enid was sorry for her _______________ (reckless, careless) and cruel words.
7. Her face grew pale and _______________ (vague, hazy, murky).
8. Yonder knights hangs his head _______________ (thoughtfully, contemplatively).
9. A low sweet voice, _______________ (trembling, quivering) with love, spoke to him.
10. You have slain this robber so _______________ (bravely, courageously).
11. Launcelot wanted to seek _______________ (amends) for the wrongs he had committed.
12. They went into a _______________ (deserted, isolated) great valley of bare stones.
13. Arthur's knights found less and less cause to prove their _______________ (skill, aptitude).

MULTIPLE CHOICE (1 pt. each)

1. Geraint comes to Arthur's court to tell him of a:
   - **a.** black deer
   - **b.** white stag
   - **c.** white brachet
2. Geraint goes to the hunt with:
   - **a.** Guinevere
   - **b.** Gawain
   - **c.** Arthur
3. Oringle is:
   - **a.** beheaded
   - **b.** rewarded
   - **c.** knighted
4. The white stag is beheaded by:
   - **a.** Geraint
   - **b.** Oringle
   - **c.** Excalibur
5. The mistress of the damsel who lures Arthur to Tarn Wathelyne:
   - **a.** Nimue
   - **b.** Allewes
   - **c.** Morgana le Fay
6. Gawain and Lady Ragnell live together for:
   - **a.** 6 years
   - **b.** 7 years
   - **c.** 8 years
7. Percivale does not see another living soul besides his mother until he is:
   - **a.** 21
   - **b.** 15
   - **c.** 5
8. Percivale's weapon of choice:
   - **a.** lance
   - **b.** dart
   - **c.** spear
9. According to the damsel in the castle, the downfall of Logres will be caused by:
   - **a.** Launcelot
   - **b.** Gawain
   - **c.** Percivale
10. The hermit who comes to Arthur's court predicts the birth of:
    - **a.** Galahad
    - **b.** Percivale
    - **c.** Mordred
11. The Grail Keeper is:
    - **a.** Naciens
    - **b.** Pelles
    - **c.** Blanchefleur
12. Launcelot cannot touch the Grail because of his:
    - **a.** anger
    - **b.** sin
    - **c.** pride
13. Galahad is raised by:
    - **a.** Elaine
    - **b.** Pelles
    - **c.** monks and nuns

QUOTATIONS (2 pts. each)

1. "I have no lady. And yet … there is none fairer that ever I have seen than this damsel your daughter, the lady Enid …"

   Who said it?____________________ To whom? ____________________

2. "This is devil's work!"

   When was this quotation spoken?____

3. "By this your choice—to leave the choice to me—you have undone the enchantment forever …"

   Who said it?____________________ To whom? ____________________

4. "In the days long past, Merlin the good enchanter told me that you would come when the highest moment of the realm of Logres drew near."

   Who said it?____________________ To whom? ____________________

5. "Alas! I have lived too long, for now I am dishonoured!"

   Who said it? ____

COMPREHENSION QUESTIONS (3 pts. each)

1. Why does Geraint tell Enid not to speak to him on their journey in the woods?

   ____

   ____

   ____

2. What quest does Gromer give to King Arthur?

   ____

   ____

   ____

3. What does Percivale get to see in the castle?

   ____

   ____

   ____

4. Why does Launcelot feel he is so dishonoured that he goes insane?

   ____

   ____

   ____

King Arthur: Book III Quiz

Name:______________________________ Date: ________________ Score: ________
60 total pts.

FACTS TO KNOW: Match each word below with the correct description. (1 pt. each)

Castle of the Maiden
Grail Maiden
Naciens
Enchanted Ship
Grail Priest
White Knight

1. ____________________ castle where the sick maiden lies
2. ____________________ hermit who raised Galahad
3. ____________________ Galahad
4. ____________________ keeper of the shield that belongs to Galahad
5. ____________________ ship that takes Dindrane and the knights to their destination
6. ____________________ Blanchefleur

VOCABULARY: Write the correct vocabulary word in the blanks below. (1 pt. each)

1. I shall ____________________ (saw, cut) you in pieces where you kneel.
2. I will make you a knight ____________________ (immediately).
3. All that night Galahad kept his ____________________ (watch, surveillance) in the chapel.
4. King Pelles spoke to Launcelot in a ____________________ (weak, frail) voice.
5. I shall go forth in quest of the Holy ____________________ (cup of Jesus).
6. A strange knight ____________________ (clothed) all in shining white armor came riding out of the forest.
7. They rode across the ____________________ (dreary, somber, depressing) uplands.
8. I shall treat you as a ____________________ (criminal, villain, lawbreaker) and a traitor.
9. In the letters' ____________________ (place, position) was a new inscription.
10. The knight shouted, "Cease this ____________________ (conflict, disagreement, contention)!"
11. Naciens gave Gawain ____________________ (forgiveness, remission of sin, relief from guilt) and counsel.
12. He is the ancient ____________________ (one who lives in solitude) of Carbonek.
13. Launcelot fell to the ground and all his senses ____________________ (abandoned, deserted) him.

MULTIPLE CHOICE (1 pt. each)

1. How many years after the death of Christ is the Siege Perilous filled?
   - **a.** 513
   - **b.** 454
   - **c.** 412
2. Galahad was a descendant of:
   - **a.** Joseph of Arimathea
   - **b.** King Arthur
   - **c.** Gawain
3. The first knight to desire to follow the quest of the Holy Grail:
   - **a.** Launcelot
   - **b.** Gawain
   - **c.** Percivale
4. Who struck Bagdemagus on his shoulder and sent him back to the abbey?
   - **a.** Naciens
   - **b.** Galahad
   - **c.** The White Knight
5. The unworthy knight who tried to take the golden crown:
   - **a.** Launcelot
   - **b.** Hector
   - **c.** Melyas
6. What animals did Percivale see fighting each other?
   - **a.** a lion and a bear
   - **b.** a serpent and a lion
   - **c.** a tiger and a serpent
7. Who was beating Sir Lionel with thorns?
   - **a.** two knights
   - **b.** three knights
   - **c.** twenty knights
8. For killing the monk Sir Lionel did penance for:
   - **a.** 1 month + 1 day
   - **b.** 6 months + 1 day
   - **c.** 1 year + 1 day
9. How did Launcelot know that he hadn't been dreaming of the Holy Grail?
   - **a.** Naciens told him.
   - **b.** Sir Percivale witnessed it.
   - **c.** His sword and helmet were gone.
10. The cure for the sick lady of the castle:
    - **a.** the love of a pure knight
    - **b.** blood from a pure virgin
    - **c.** Galahad's arrival
11. On his quest for the Holy Grail, Gawain first met:
    - **a.** Sir Launcelot
    - **b.** Sir Hector
    - **c.** Sir Galahad
12. Who was lying in the great hall at Castle Carbonek?
    - **a.** Blanchefleur
    - **b.** King Arthur
    - **c.** King Pelles
13. Against whom did Naciens sin, which resulted in his long life?
    - **a.** Merlin
    - **b.** Nimue
    - **c.** Joseph of Arimathea
14. Who joined Percivale and Blanchefleur in marriage?
    - **a.** King Arthur
    - **b.** Galahad
    - **c.** King Pelles
15. Who told King Arthur the story of the quest of the Holy Grail?
    - **a.** Sir Gawain
    - **b.** Sir Bors
    - **c.** Sir Launcelot

QUOTATIONS (2 pts. each)

1. "Sir, this is not my sword, nor am I worthy to wear it at my side. Evil shall come to any who seeks to draw it knowing that he is not worthy …"

   Who said it? ______________________ To whom? ______________________

2. "Now blessed be the good fortune that brings this shield to me."

   Who said it? ______________________ To whom? ______________________

3. "I give you my word that never again will I feel envy towards Sir Galahad."

   Who said it? ______________________ To whom? ______________________

4. "Go forward in the fear of God, and live to tell of the ending of the quest of the Holy Grail …"

   Who said it? ______________________ To whom? ______________________

5. "Alas, all my great deeds of arms have I done for the sake of Queen Guinevere, without stopping to think if they were right or wrong."

   Who said it? ______________________ To whom? ______________________

6. "So shall the darkness fall upon Logres."

   Who thought it? ____________ What was he witnessing? ______________________________

7. "And when he died this penance was laid on me: that I should live beyond the span of mortal men to be the Priest of the Grail until the coming of Sir Galahad the Good Knight."

   Who said it? ______________________ To whom? ______________________

COMPREHENSION QUESTIONS (3 pts. each)

1. What is the history of the sword Galahad pulls from the stone?

   ____

2. What does the White Knight tell Galahad concerning the history of the shield?

   ____

   ____

3. What happens to Dindrane?

   ____

   ____

4. How does Gawain take away the Curse of Desolation from Carbonek?

   ____

   ____

King Arthur: Book IV Quiz

Name:______________________________ Date: ________________ Score: ________

43 total pts.

FACTS TO KNOW: Match each word below with the correct description. (1 pt. each)

Archbishop of Canterbury	Colgrevaunce	Mordred
Bedivere	Melliagraunce	Tower of London

1. ____________________ the only surviving knight to keep the legend of Logres alive
2. ____________________ place of imprisonment for British royalty
3. ____________________ the most evil knight in Logres
4. ____________________ knight involved in Mordred's conspiracy
5. ____________________ son of Bagdemagus
6. ____________________ high-ranking official of the church of England

VOCABULARY: Write the correct vocabulary word in the blanks below. (1 pt. each)

1. Gawain ____________________ (worried, fretted, stewed) on his brothers' deaths.
2. Agravain was jealous of Sir Launcelot's fame and ____________________ (fame, celebrity).
3. Mordred was ____________________ (raiding, pillaging) the lands of all who would not fight for him.
4. King Arthur found Gawain lying ____________________ (fatally) wounded.
5. Sir Mordred brought ____________________ (strife, conflict, disagreement) to the whole realm of Logres.
6. Launcelot was the ____________________ (most patient, humble, passive) and most gentle among ladies.
7. Melliagraunce ____________________ (strutted) about, boasting that he was the best knight.
8. The evening fell, dark and ____________________ (menacing, threatening).
9. You have come to me with lies and ____________________ (malicious falsehoods) in your mouths.
10. Leave your weeping, for it is of no ____________________ (help, benefit) —and my time is short.

MULTIPLE CHOICE (1 pt. each)

1. How many of King Arthur's knights tried unsuccessfully to heal Sir Urry?
   - **a.** 100 knights
   - **b.** 110 knights
   - **c.** 120 knights
2. How did Launcelot free himself from Melliagraunce's dungeon?
   - **a.** He crosses himself
   - **b.** He fights the guards
   - **c.** He kisses the damsel
3. How many knights did King Arthur send to seize Launcelot in Guinevere's room?
   - **a.** 10 knights
   - **b.** 12 knights
   - **c.** 20 knights
4. Who advised Launcelot against visiting the queen in her room?
   - **a.** Sir Gawain
   - **b.** Sir Gareth
   - **c.** Sir Bors
5. Who ruled Britain in King Arthur's absence?
   - **a.** Launcelot
   - **b.** Bors
   - **c.** Mordred
6. To where did Guinevere escape from Mordred?
   - **a.** Tower of London
   - **b.** Avalon
   - **c.** Canterbury
7. Who warned King Arthur to make a truce with Mordred?
   - **a.** Gawain
   - **b.** Sir Bors
   - **c.** Launcelot
8. Why was King Arthur carried away in the barge?
   - **a.** so his wound would heal
   - **b.** to escape the Saxons
   - **c.** to escape Launcelot
9. After Launcelot's death, where do Hector and Bors go?
   - **a.** to Camelot
   - **b.** to France
   - **c.** to the Holy Land

QUOTATIONS (2 pts. each)

1. "Come out and fight, and all your treacherous curs with you—for here am I, Sir Launcelot of the Lake, ready to do battle with you all!"

   Who said it? ______________________ To whom? ______________________

2. "… here now you lie dying, the man whom I loved best in all the world. … For you and Launcelot I loved best of all my knights: and I have lost you both."

   Who said it? ______________________ To whom? ______________________

3. "But be you sure that I will come again when the land of Britain has need of me, and the realm of Logres shall rise once more out of the darkness."

   Who said it? ______________________ To whom? ______________________

COMPREHENSION QUESTIONS (3 pts. each)

1. What reminds King Arthur that Logres will soon fall?

2. What is Gawain's last request?

3. How does the battle with Mordred begin?

4. What do Guinevere and Launcelot do to repent of their sins?

King Arthur: Final Exam

Name:____________________________________ Date: __________________ Score: _________
135 total pts.

READING NOTES: Match each word below with the correct description. (1 pt. each)

Avalon	Camelot	Grail Priest	Logres	Tintagel
Balan	Castle Carbonek	Hector	Mordred	Uther Pendragon
Balyn	Elaine of Astolat	King Pant & Elayne	Naciens	
Bedivere	Enchanted Ship	Lady Liones	Saxons	
Blanchefleur	Excalibur	Lady Ragnell	Sir Bernlak	

1. ________________________ place where the Holy Grail resides; place of the Dolorous Stroke

2. ________________________ king and queen of North Wales; parents of Launcelot

3. ________________________ brother of Balyn; the one Balyn loved most in the world

4. ________________________ Germanic tribe that invaded Britain in the 5th & 6th centuries

5. ________________________ name of Arthur's kingdom

6. ________________________ capital of Arthur's kingdom; modern-day Winchester, England

7. ________________________ the sword of Arthur

8. ________________________ king of Briton; father of Arthur

9. ________________________ knight who struck the Dolorous Stroke

10. ________________________ Land of Mystery; place where Merlin took Arthur as an infant

11. ________________________ King Mark's castle in Cornwall; castle where Igrayne was tricked by Uther

12. ________________________ Launcelot's half-brother

13. ________________________ Knight of the Lake; the Green Knight

14. ________________________ sister of Lady Linnet; practices evil magic

15. ________________________ Percivale's love

16. ________________________ under the curse of Morgana; marries Gawain

17. ________________________ daughter of King Pelles; in love with Launcelot

18. ________________________ hermit who raised Galahad

19. ________________________ Galahad

20. ________________________ ship that takes Dindrane and the knights to their destination

21. ________________________ the only surviving knight to keep the legend of Logres alive

22. ________________________ the most evil knight in Logres

VOCABULARY: Write the correct vocabulary word in the blanks below. (1 pt. each)

________	1. avail	A.	criminal, villain, lawbreaker
________	2. ominous	B.	strife, conflict, disagreement
________	3. slander	C.	encouraged, nurtured
________	4. dissension	D.	abandoned, deserted
________	5. renown	E.	to aid, assist, relieve
________	6. feeble	F.	contemptuously, disdainfully
________	7. forsook	G.	vague, hazy, murky
________	8. felon	H.	miserable, woeful
________	9. hermit	I.	to help, benefit
________	10. vigil	J.	malicious falsehood
________	11. dire	K.	weak, frail
________	12. mortally	L.	fatally
________	13. festered	M.	one who lives in solitude
________	14. fostered	N.	menacing, threatening
________	15. scornfully	O.	urgent, fearful
________	16. indistinct	P.	a watch, surveillance
________	17. wretched	Q.	fame, celebrity
________	18. succour	R.	became infected, rotted

MULTIPLE CHOICE (1 pt. each)

1. King Arthur's foster father is:
- **a.** Sir Ector
- **b.** Sir Gawain
- **c.** Uther

2. Balan does not recognize Balyn because he does not have his own:
- **a.** shield
- **b.** sword
- **c.** armor

3. Merlin says the person who will bring about the downfall of Logres is:
- **a.** Launcelot
- **b.** Guinevere
- **c.** Morgana

4. The knight whose coming to the Round Table signifies one year before the Holy Grail comes is:
- **a.** Gawain
- **b.** Launcelot
- **c.** Percivale

5. The best knight of all will sit in the:
   a. Siege Perilous
   b. Siege Dangerous
   c. Siege Sinister
6. The Green Knight has come to Arthur's court to test the Round Table's:
   a. strength
   b. skill
   c. bravery
7. The person who sent the Green Knight to Arthur's court:
   a. Merlin
   b. Morgana
   c. Nimue
8. The chapel where Launcelot has to go to save the injured knight is the Chapel____________.
   a. Perilous
   b. Dangerous
   c. Dolorous
9. Sir Gareth's brother:
   a. Gawain
   b. Launcelot
   c. The Red Knight
10. The best knight Launcelot has ever jousted with:
    a. Gawain
    b. Percivale
    c. Tristram
11. To avenge the death of her brother, Queen Isaud keeps:
    a. a dragon's tooth
    b. a piece of a shirt
    c. a sword chip
12. Geraint goes to the hunt with:
    a. Guinevere
    b. Gawain
    c. Arthur
13. Oringle is:
    a. beheaded
    b. rewarded
    c. knighted
14. The mistress of the damsel who lures Arthur to Tarn Wathelyne:
    a. Nimue
    b. Allewes
    c. Morgana le Fay
15. Percivale does not see another living soul besides his mother until he is:
    a. 21
    b. 15
    c. 5
16. According to the damsel in the castle, the downfall of Logres will be caused by:
    a. Launcelot
    b. Gawain
    c. Percivale
17. The hermit who comes to Arthur's court predicts the birth of:
    a. Galahad
    b. Percivale
    c. Mordred
18. Launcelot cannot touch the Grail because of his:
    a. anger
    b. sin
    c. pride
19. Galahad was a descendant of:
    a. Joseph of Arimathea
    b. King Arthur
    c. Gawain
20. The unworthy knight who tries to take the golden crown:
    a. Launcelot
    b. Hector
    c. Melyas

21. For killing the monk Sir Lionel does penance for:

a. 1 month + 1 day

b. 6 months + 1 day

c. 1 year + 1 day

22. The cure for the sick lady of the castle:

a. the love of a pure knight

b. blood from a pure virgin

c. Galahad's arrival

23. Who was lying in the great hall at Castle Carbonek?

a. Blanchefleur

b. King Arthur

c. King Pelles

24. Against whom did Naciens sin, which results in his long life?

a. Merlin

b. Nimue

c. Joseph of Arimathea

25. Who joins Percivale and Blanchefleur in marriage?

a. King Arthur

b. Galahad

c. King Pelles

26. How does Launcelot free himself from Melliagraunce's dungeon?

a. He crosses himself.

b. He fights the guards.

c. He kisses the damsel.

27. Who advises Launcelot against visiting the queen in her room?

a. Sir Gawain

b. Sir Gareth

c. Sir Bors

28. Who rules Britain in King Arthur's absence?

a. Launcelot

b. Bors

c. Mordred

29. To where does Guinevere escape from Mordred?

a. Tower of London

b. Avalon

c. Canterbury

30. After Launcelot's death, where do Hector and Bors go?

a. to Camelot

b. to France

c. to the Holy Land

QUOTATIONS (2 pts. each)

1. "A little while after his birth at dark Tintagel, Uther, who hearkened to my words, gave the child into my care, and I bore him to Avalon, the Land of Mystery."

Who said it? ________________________________ To whom? ______________________________

2. "Bury us, I pray you, in the same tomb, and write upon it that here lie two brothers who slew one another by mischance …"

Who said it? ________________________________ To whom? ______________________________

3. "Yet I would that you loved another; for by her very beauty shall come the end of Logres."

Who said it? ________________________________ To whom? ______________________________

4. "A knight without mercy is dishonoured: but to kill a fair lady is shame unto the world's end!"

Who said it? ________________________________ To whom? ______________________________

5. "For though I lack a weapon, yet shall I lack no honour—and if you slay me weaponless, it is you who will be shamed."

Who said it? ______________________ To whom? ______________________

6. "I have loved her long, and she me. And I promised to fight and slay whom she would, even though it were Arthur the King."

Who said it? ______________________ To whom? ______________________

7. "As for the lace, you hid it but for love of your life—and that is a little sin, and for it I pardon you."

Who said it? ______________________ To whom? ______________________

8. "Merlin has spoken his name to you—and see, that name grows in letters of gold upon the empty siege on the right hand of the Siege Perilous!"

Who said it? ______________________ To whom? ______________________

9. "When you are a noble knight of noble birth, you shall have my love—but not before!"

Who said it? ______________________ To whom? ______________________

10. "Only Launcelot bowed his head in his hands, and the tears ran between his fingers as he thought of his own love for Guinevere."

Why does Launcelot cry? ____

11. "I have no lady. And yet … there is none fairer that ever I have seen than this damsel your daughter, the lady Enid … "

Who said it? ______________________ To whom? ______________________

12. "This is devil's work!"

When was this spoken? ____

13. "By this your choice—to leave the choice to me—you have undone the enchantment forever …"

Who said it? ______________________ To whom? ______________________

14. "In the days long past, Merlin the good enchanter told me that you would come when the highest moment of the realm of Logres drew near."

Who said it? ______________________ To whom? ______________________

15. "Alas! I have lived too long, for now I am dishonoured!"

Who said it? ____

16. "Sir, this is not my sword, nor am I worthy to wear it at my side. Evil shall come to any who seeks to draw it knowing that he is not worthy ..."

Who said it? ______________________________ To whom? ____________________________

17. "Now blessed be the good fortune that brings this shield to me."

Who said it? ______________________________ To whom? ____________________________

18. "I give you my word that never again will I feel envy towards Sir Galahad."

Who said it? ______________________________ To whom? ____________________________

19. "Go forward in the fear of God, and live to tell of the ending of the quest of the Holy Grail ..."

Who said it? ______________________________ To whom? ____________________________

20. "Alas, all my great deeds of arms have I done for the sake of Queen Guinevere, without stopping to think if they were right or wrong."

Who said it? ______________________________ To whom? ____________________________

21. "So shall the darkness fall upon Logres."

Who thought it? ____________________

What was he witnessing?____

22. "And when he died, this penance was laid on me: that I should live beyond the span of mortal men to be the Priest of the Grail until the coming of Sir Galahad the Good Knight."

Who said it? ______________________________ To whom? ____________________________

23. "Come out and fight, and all your treacherous curs with you—for here am I, Sir Launcelot of the Lake, ready to do battle with you all!"

Who said it? ____________________ Where was he?_____________________________________

24. "... here now you lie dying, the man whom I loved best in all the world. ... For you and Launcelot I loved best of all my knights: and I have lost you both."

Who said it? ______________________________ To whom? ____________________________

25. "But be you sure that I will come again when the land of Britain has need of me, and the realm of Logres shall rise once more out of the darkness."

Who said it? ______________________________ To whom? ____________________________

ESSAY (15 pts.)

Describe Launcelot's struggle with good and evil. This should include the cause of his struggle, his attempts to live a virtuous life, his failures, and their consequences.

King Arthur: Book I Quiz KEY

Name:______________________ Date: ______________ Score: ________
64 total pts.

FACTS TO KNOW: Match each word below with the correctdescription. (1 pt. each)

Avalon	Castle Carbonek	Holy Grail	King Pellinore	Saxons
Balan	Excaliber	Igrayne	King Ryon	Sir Accolon
Balyn	Garlon	King Pant & Elayne	King Urience	Sir Uwaine
Camelot	Gawain	King Pelles	Logres	Uther Pendragon

1. Castle Carbonek place where the Holy Grail resides; place of the Dolorous Stroke
2. King Pellinore has the quest of the Questing Beast
3. King Pant & Elayne king and queen of North Wales; parents of Launcelot
4. Garlon the invisible knight
5. Balan brother of Balyn; the one Balyn loved most in the world
6. Saxons Germanic tribe that invaded Britain in the 5th & 6th centuries
7. Logres name of Arthur's kingdom
8. King Ryon cruel king of North Wales
9. King Urience husband of Morgana
10. Camelot capital of Arthur's kingdom; modern-day Winchester, England
11. Holy Grail the cup Jesus drank from at the Last Supper
12. Sir Uwaine son of Morgana and Urience
13. Excalibur the sword of Arthur
14. Uther Pendragon king of Briton; father of Arthur
15. King Pelles king of Castle Carbonek; victim of the Dolorous Stroke
16. Gawain son of Lot and Morgawse; nephew of Arthur
17. Balyn knight who struck the Dolorous Stroke
18. Avalon Land of Mystery; place where Merlin took Arthur as an infant
19. Sir Accolon Arthur's knight who loves Morgana le Fay
20. Igrayne wife of Gorlois, then Uther; mother of Arthur, Morgawse, Elaine, & Margana

VOCABULARY: Write the correct vocabulary word in the blanks below. (1 pt. each)

1. Set a rich ___pavilion___ (ornate tent) over the stone.
2. Merlin told the knights to go out to ___succour___ (aid, assist) gentlewomen.
3. You may ___redeem___ (retrieve) your honor by some brave deed.
4. Sir Ector bowed his head in ___reverence___ (awe, respect) before Arthur.
5. "I am going to hit you again!" ___taunted___ (jeered, ridiculed) Sir Accolon.
6. The damsel made many ___lamentations___ (expressions of grief) in her sorrow.
7. Yield you to me as ___craven___ (cowardly) and vanquished.
8. The knights did ___homage___ (special honor) to Arthur, swearing to serve and obey him.
9. We lay this ___penance___ (contrition, remorse) upon you, that you bear the body.
10. Upon every ___siege___ (seat, chair) at the table was the name of the knight in letters of gold.

MULTIPLE CHOICE: Circle the correct answer. (1 pt. each)

1. King Arthur's foster father:
   - **a.** Sir Ector
   - **b.** Sir Gawain
   - **c.** Uther
2. Balyn kills the Lady of the Lake by:
   - **a.** beheading her
   - **b.** stabbing her heart
   - **c.** shooting her with an arrow
3. Arthur has to fight a war against:
   - **a.** 10 kings
   - **b.** 12 kings
   - **c.** 15 kings
4. Balan does not recognize Balyn because he does not have his own:
   - **a.** shield
   - **b.** sword
   - **c.** armor
5. Merlin says the person who will bring about the downfall of Logres is:
   - **a.** Launcelot
   - **b.** Guinevere
   - **c.** Morgana
6. The knight whose coming to the Round Table signifies one year before the Holy Grail comes:
   - **a.** Gawain
   - **b.** Launcelot
   - **c.** Percivale
7. The best knight of all will sit in the:
   - **a.** Siege Perilous
   - **b.** Siege Dangerous
   - **c.** Siege Sinister
8. Gawain learns from his quest to:
   - **a.** always be merciful
   - **b.** joust
   - **c.** never ignore a cry for help
9. Who buries Merlin while he is still alive?
   - **a.** Morgana
   - **b.** Lady Nimue
   - **c.** Elayne
10. Where was Arthur when he woke from his deep sleep upon the boat?
    - **a.** Camelot
    - **b.** beside a deep well
    - **c.** Sir Damas' castle

QUOTATIONS (2 pts. each)

1. "A little while after his birth at dark Tintagel, Uther, who hearkened to my words, gave the child into my care, and I bore him to Avalon, the Land of Mystery."

   Who said it? Merlin To whom? angry kings and knights

2. "Bury us, I pray you, in the same tomb, and write upon it that here lie two brothers who slew one another by mischance …"

   Who said it? Balan To whom? Lady of the Castle

3. "Yet I would that you loved another; for by her very beauty shall come the end of Logres."

   Who said it? Merlin To whom? Arthur

4. "A knight without mercy is dishonoured: but to kill a fair lady is shame unto the world's end!"

   Who said it? four armed knights To whom? Gawain

5. "For though I lack a weapon, yet shall I lack no honour—and if you slay me weaponless, it is you who will be shamed."

   Who said it? Arthur To whom? Sir Accolon

6. "I have loved her long, and she me. And I promised to fight and slay whom she would, even though it were Arthur the King."

   Who said it? Sir Accolon To whom? Arthur

COMPREHENSION QUESTIONS (3 pts. each)

1. What is Arthur's first goal as king?

   He plans to drive the Saxons out of Britain.

2. Why is it called the "Dolorous Stroke" when Balyn strikes Pelles?

   Balyn is not worthy to touch the Holy Lance.

3. What is the purpose of the round table?

   The purpose of the round table is to end the quarreling of the knights as to who would get the best seat.

4. What happens to Excalibur's scabbard?

   Morgana steals it while Arthur sleeps. She then throws it into a lake, where it sinks.

King Arthur: Book II, Chapters 1-4 Quiz KEY

Name:______________________ Date: ______________ Score: ________
60 total pts.

FACTS TO KNOW: Match each word below with the correct description. (1 pt. each)

Allewes	King Mark	Lionel	Sir Bernlak
Castle Dangerous	King Rivalin	Mordred	Sir Gareth
Hector	Lady Linnet	Morgan the Wicked	Sir Ironside
King Gurman	Lady Liones	Rual	Tintagel

1. Sir Gareth brother of Gawain, Gaheris, and Agravaine; Knight of the Kitchen
2. Mordred son of Morgana le Fay; Arthur's nephew
3. Morgan the Wicked killer of Rivalin and usurper of his throne
4. Castle Dangerous name of castle the Red Knight is besieging; home of Lady Liones
5. Tintagel King Mark's castle in Cornwall; castle where Igrayne was tricked by Uther
6. Lionel Launcelot's cousin
7. Hector Launcelot's half-brother
8. King Rivalin father of Tristram; king of Lyonesse
9. Sir Bernlak Knight of the Lake; the Green Knight
10. Sir Ironside Red Knight; under the spell of Morgana le Fay
11. King Gurman king of Ireland; father of Iseult
12. Allewes evil sorceress; companion of Morgana le Fay
13. King Mark king of Cornwall; Tristram's uncle
14. Lady Liones sister of Lady Linnet; practices evil magic
15. Rual servant of Rivalin who raises Tristram
16. Lady Linnet damsel in distress; needs aid of Arthur's knights

VOCABULARY: Write the correct vocabulary word in the blanks below. (1 pt. each)

1. I am no scullion, and of nobler ancestry (lineage) than you are!
2. The green knight cast some dire (fearful, ominous) enchantment upon everyone.
3. Bestow (to confer, place) upon him the high order of knighthood.
4. It's only a wretched (miserable, woeful) kitchen knave.
5. They could not restrain (hold back) the tears from running down their cheeks.
6. Tristram's wound festered (became infected, rotted, decayed) and might not be cured.
7. Lady Linnet laughed aloud in mockery (ridicule, derision) at Gareth.
8. The child was lovingly fostered (encouraged, nurtured, cared for) by his parents.
9. You are uncourteous so to rebuke (reprove, criticize) me and mock at me.
10. Launcelot was the peerless (unequalled) knight of whom Merlin had spoken.

MULTIPLE CHOICE (1 pt. each)

1. The Green Knight has come to Arthur's court to test the Round Table's:
   - **a.** strength
   - **b.** skill
   - **c.** bravery
2. Gawain is to look for the Green Knight in:
   - **a.** 1 month
   - **b.** 1 year + 1 day
   - **c.** 6 months + 1 day
3. The person who sent the Green Knight to Arthur's court was:
   - **a.** Merlin
   - **b.** Morgana
   - **c.** Nimue
4. Launcelot chooses a dungeon over:
   - **a.** death by sword
   - **b.** four beautiful women
   - **c.** thirty black knights
5. Morgana's servant cries when releasing Launcelot because she:
   - **a.** loves him
   - **b.** is afraid he will die
   - **c.** hates him
6. The chapel where Launcelot has to go to save the injured knight is the Chapel__________.
   - **a.** Perilous
   - **b.** Dangerous
   - **c.** Dolorous
7. The third gift the Knight of the Kitchen requests is to be knighted by:
   - **a.** Gawain
   - **b.** Arthur
   - **c.** Launcelot
8. The Knight of the Kitchen gets his sword from:
   - **a.** Launcelot
   - **b.** a dwarf
   - **c.** Gawain
9. Sir Gareth's brother is:
   - **a.** Gawain
   - **b.** Launcelot
   - **c.** The Red Knight
10. Lady Liones marries:
    - **a.** Gareth
    - **b.** Gaheris
    - **c.** Gawain

11. The best knight Launcelot has ever jousted with is:
   a. Gawain
   b. Percivale
   c. Tristram

12. To save thirty lads of Cornwall, Tristram fights and kills:
   a. Morgan
   b. Marhault
   c. Mordred

13. To avenge the death of her brother, Queen Isaud keeps:
   a. A dragon's tooth
   b. A piece of a shirt
   c. A sword chip

14. When Mark finds out Tristram and Iseult love each other, Tristram is:
   a. Beheaded
   b. Put in prison
   c. Banished

QUOTATIONS (2 pts. each)

1. "As for the lace, you hid it but for love of your life—and that is a little sin, and for it I pardon you."

   Who said it? Sir Bernlak To whom? Gawain

2. "Merlin has spoken his name to you—and see, that name grows in letters of gold upon the empty siege on the right hand of the Siege Perilous!"

   Who said it? Lady Nimue To whom? Arthur

3. "When you are a noble knight of noble birth, you shall have my love—but not before!"

   Who said it? Lady Liones To whom? Sir Gareth

4. "Only Launcelot bowed his head in his hands, and the tears ran between his fingers as he thought of his own love for Guinevere."

   Why does Launcelot cry? Launcelot cries because he knows exactly how Tristram feels.

COMPREHENSION QUESTIONS (3 pts. each)

1. What is the challenge posed by the Green Knight, and who accepts it?

   If any man is brave enough to exchange stroke for stroke, the Green Knight will give him an axe. Sir Gawain accepts the challenge.

2. Launcelot faces three perils at the Chapel Perilous before he can come safely away with the sword and cloth. Name the three perils.

   Launcelot faces 30 great black knights, an earthquake (or moving floor), and Sorceress Allewes wanted a kiss.

3. Why does Lady Linnet begin to think Gareth may be of noble birth?

She is surprised that he defends her even though she insults him continuously.

4. How does Iseult discover Tristram's true identity?

She matches the piece of metal from Marhault's head with the missing piece from Tristram's sword.

King Arthur: Book II, Chapters 5-8 Quiz KEY

Name:_______________________________ Date: ______________ Score: __________
57 total pts.

FACTS TO KNOW: Match each word below with the correct description. (1 pt. each)

Blanchefleur	Duke Liconal	Elaine of Astolat	Lady Ragnell	Sir Oringle
Dolorous Lady	Duke Yder	Gromer Somer Joure	Sir Gonemans	

1. Gromer Somer Joure the giant knight who struck fear into anyone who approached
2. Sir Oringle evil knight who struck Enid in the face
3. Blanchefleur Percivale's love
4. Dolorous Lady imprisoned in scalding water by Morgana le Fay
5. Sir Gonemans Percivale's tutor in the art of knighthood
6. Lady Ragnell under the curse of Morgana; marries Gawain
7. Duke Liconal knight who withheld nephew's inheritance from him
8. Elaine of Astolat daughter of King Pelles; in love with Launcelot
9. Duke Yder rightful heir of Duke Liconal's dukedom

VOCABULARY: Write the correct vocabulary word in the blanks below. (1 pt. each)

1. A vile churl (crude, ill-bred person) this dwarf is!
2. He turned away with a cry of anguish (torment, distress).
3. A damsel lay sleeping on a couch of rich silk and samite (silken cloth).
4. Elaine prospered (succeeded) not at all in her love.
5. Percivale looked scornfully (disdainfully, contemptuously) at Sir Kay.
6. Enid was sorry for her rash (reckless, careless) and cruel words.
7. Her face grew pale and indistinct (vague, hazy, murky).
8. Yonder knights hangs his head pensively (thoughtfully, contemplatively).
9. A low sweet voice, tremulous (trembling, quivering) with love, spoke to him.
10. You have slain this robber so valiantly (bravely, courageously).
11. Launcelot wanted to seek redress (amends) for the wrongs he had committed.
12. They went into a desolate (deserted, isolated) great valley of bare stones.
13. Arthur's knights found less and less cause to prove their prowess (skill, aptitude).

MULTIPLE CHOICE (1 pt. each)

1. Geraint comes to Arthur's court to tell him of a:
   - a. black deer
   - b. white stag
   - c. white brachet
2. Geraint goes to the hunt with:
   - a. Guinevere
   - b. Gawain
   - c. Arthur
3. Oringle is:
   - a. beheaded
   - b. rewarded
   - c. knighted
4. The white stag is beheaded by:
   - a. Geraint
   - b. Oringle
   - c. Excalibur
5. The mistress of the damsel who lures Arthur to Tarn Wathelyne:
   - a. Nimue
   - b. Allewes
   - c. Morgana le Fay
6. Gawain and Lady Ragnell live together for:
   - a. 6 years
   - b. 7 years
   - c. 8 years
7. Percivale does not see another living soul besides his mother until he is:
   - a. 21
   - b. 15
   - c. 5
8. Percivale's weapon of choice:
   - a. lance
   - b. dart
   - c. spear
9. According to the damsel in the castle, the downfall of Logres will be caused by:
   - a. Launcelot
   - b. Gawain
   - c. Percivale
10. The hermit who comes to Arthur's court predicts the birth of:
    - a. Galahad
    - b. Percivale
    - c. Mordred
11. The Grail Keeper is:
    - a. Naciens
    - b. Pelles
    - c. Blanchefleur
12. Launcelot cannot touch the Grail because of his:
    - a. anger
    - b. sin
    - c. pride
13. Galahad is raised by:
    - a. Elaine
    - b. Pelles
    - c. monks and nuns

QUOTATIONS (2 pts. each)

1. "I have no lady. And yet … there is none fairer that ever I have seen than this damsel your daughter, the lady Enid …"

   Who said it? Geraint To whom? Duke Liconal

2. "This is devil's work!"

   When was this quotation spoken? It was spoken when Arthur charged at Gromer Somer Joure.

3. "By this your choice - to leave the choice to me—you have undone the enchantment forever …"

   Who said it? Ragnell To whom? Gawain

4. "In the days long past, Merlin the good enchanter told me that you would come when the highest moment of the realm of Logres drew near."

   Who said it? Arthur To whom? Percivale

5. "Alas! I have lived too long, for now I am dishonoured!"

   Who said it? Launcelot

COMPREHENSION QUESTIONS (3 pts. each)

1. Why does Geraint tell Enid not to speak to him on their journey in the woods?

   She insults him when she finds out that he is not a knight, and he is angry with her.

2. What quest does Gromer give to King Arthur?

   He tells Arthur to ask all the women he meets what it is that women most desire. After a year and one day, Arthur is to return and give his answer.

3. What does Percivale get to see in the castle?

   He sees a damsel carrying a covered grail, a damsel carrying a plate, and a damsel carrying a spear dripping with blood.

4. Why does Launcelot feel he is so dishonored that he goes insane?

   Launcelot marries Elaine thinking she is Guinevere. This is a betrayal of Arthur because Launcelot thinks Elaine is the wife of his king, and it is a betrayal of his love for Guinevere because he married another woman.

King Arthur: Book III Quiz KEY

Name:______________________________ Date: ______________ Score: ________
60 total pts.

FACTS TO KNOW: Match each word below with the correct description. (1 pt. each)

Castle of the Maiden	Grail Maiden	Naciens
Enchanted Ship	Grail Priest	White Knight

1. Castle of the Maiden castle where the sick maiden lies
2. Naciens hermit who raised Galahad
3. Grail Priest Galahad
4. White Knight keeper of the shield that belongs to Galahad
5. Enchanted Ship ship that takes Dindrane and the knights to their destination
6. Grail Maiden Blanchefleur

VOCABULARY: Write the correct vocabulary word in the blanks below. (1 pt. each)

1. I shall hew (saw, cut) you in pieces where you kneel.
2. I will make you a knight forthwith (immediately).
3. All that night Galahad kept his vigil (watch, surveillance) in the chapel.
4. King Pelles spoke to Launcelot in a feeble (weak, frail) voice.
5. I shall go forth in quest of the Holy Grail (cup of Jesus).
6. A strange knight clad (clothed) all in shining white armor came riding out of the forest.
7. They rode across the bleak (dreary, somber, depressing) uplands.
8. I shall treat you as a felon (criminal, villain, lawbreaker) and a traitor.
9. In the letters' stead (place, position) was a new inscription.
10. The knight shouted, "Cease this strife (conflict, disagreement, contention)!"
11. Naciens gave Gawain absolution (forgiveness, remission of sin, relief from guilt) and counsel.
12. He is the ancient hermit (one who lives in solitude) of Carbonek.
13. Launcelot fell to the ground and all his senses forsook (abandoned, deserted) him.

MULTIPLE CHOICE (1 pt. each)

1. How many years after the death of Christ is the Siege Perilous filled?
   - a. 513
   - b. 454
   - c. 412
2. Galahad was a descendant of:
   - a. Joseph of Arimathea
   - b. King Arthur
   - c. Gawain
3. The first knight to desire to follow the quest of the Holy Grail:
   - a. Launcelot
   - b. Gawain
   - c. Percivale
4. Who struck Bagdemagus on his shoulder and sent him back to the abbey?
   - a. Naciens
   - b. Galahad
   - c. The White Knight
5. The unworthy knight who tried to take the golden crown:
   - a. Launcelot
   - b. Hector
   - c. Melyas
6. What animals did Percivale see fighting each other?
   - a. a lion and a bear
   - b. a serpent and a lion
   - c. a tiger and a serpent
7. Who was beating Sir Lionel with thorns?
   - a. two knights
   - b. three knights
   - c. twenty knights
8. For killing the monk Sir Lionel did penance for:
   - a. 1 month + 1 day
   - b. 6 months + 1 day
   - c. 1 year + 1 day
9. How did Launcelot know that he hadn't been dreaming of the Holy Grail?
   - a. Naciens told him.
   - b. Sir Percivale witnessed it.
   - c. His sword and helmet were gone.
10. The cure for the sick lady of the castle:
    - a. the love of a pure knight
    - b. blood from a pure virgin
    - c. Galahad's arrival
11. On his quest for the Holy Grail, Gawain first met:
    - a. Sir Launcelot
    - b. Sir Hector
    - c. Sir Galahad
12. Who was lying in the great hall at Castle Carbonek?
    - a. Blanchefleur
    - b. King Arthur
    - c. King Pelles
13. Against whom did Naciens sin, which resulted in his long life?
    - a. Merlin
    - b. Nimue
    - c. Joseph of Arimathea
14. Who joined Percivale and Blanchefleur in marriage?
    - a. King Arthur
    - b. Galahad
    - c. King Pelles
15. Who told King Arthur the story of the quest of the Holy Grail?
    - a. Sir Gawain
    - b. Sir Bors
    - c. Sir Launcelot

QUOTATIONS (2 pts. each)

1. "Sir, this is not my sword, nor am I worthy to wear it at my side. Evil shall come to any who seeks to draw it knowing that he is not worthy …"

   Who said it? Launcelot To whom? Arthur

2. "Now blessed be the good fortune that brings this shield to me."

   Who said it? Galahad To whom? The squire

3. "I give you my word that never again will I feel envy towards Sir Galahad."

   Who said it? Percivale To whom? The hermit

4. "Go forward in the fear of God, and live to tell of the ending of the quest of the Holy Grail …"

   Who said it? Naciens To whom? Sir Bors

5. "Alas, all my great deeds of arms have I done for the sake of Queen Guinevere, without stopping to think if they were right or wrong."

   Who said it? Launcelot To whom? Naciens

6. "So shall the darkness fall upon Logres."

   Who thought it? Gawain What was he witnessing? He was witnessing a hand putting out the candles.

7. "And when he died this penance was laid on me: that I should live beyond the span of mortal men to be the Priest of the Grail until the coming of Sir Galahad the Good Knight."

   Who said it? Naciens To whom? Gawain

COMPREHENSION QUESTIONS (3 pts. each)

1. What is the history of the sword Galahad pulls from the stone?

   It is the sword that Balyn used to kill his brother Balan.

2. What does the White Knight tell Galahad concerning the history of the shield?

   Made in the Holy Land, the shield was brought by Joseph of Arimathea to Britain. The cross was painted with his blood.

3. What happens to Dindrane?

   Dindrane gives blood and heals the sick maiden. She bleeds to death and is placed upon the Enchanted Ship.

4. How does Gawain take away the Curse of Desolation from Carbonek?

   Gawain resists temptation and asks about the meaning of the procession.

King Arthur: Book IV Quiz KEY

Name:______________________ Date: ______________ Score: __________
43 total pts.

FACTS TO KNOW: Match each word below with the correct description. (1 pt. each)

Archbishop of Canterbury	Colgrevaunce	Mordred
Bedivere	Melliagraunce	Tower of London

1. Bedivere the only surviving knight to keep the legend of Logres alive
2. Tower of London place of imprisonment for British royalty
3. Mordred the most evil knight in Logres
4. Colgrevaunce knight involved in Mordred's conspiracy
5. Melliagraunce son of Bagdemagus
6. Archbishop of Canterbury high-ranking official of the church of England

VOCABULARY: Write the correct vocabulary word in the blanks below. (1 pt. each)

1. Gawain brooded (worried, fretted, stewed) on his brothers' deaths.
2. Agravain was jealous of Sir Launcelot's fame and renown (fame, celebrity).
3. Mordred was harrying (raiding, pillaging) the lands of all who would not fight for him.
4. King Arthur found Gawain lying mortally (fatally) wounded.
5. Sir Mordred brought dissension (strife, conflict, disagreement) to the whole realm of Logres.
6. Launcelot was the meekest (most patient, humble, passive) and most gentle among ladies.
7. Melliagraunce swaggered (strutted) about, boasting that he was the best knight.
8. The evening fell, dark and ominous (menacing, threatening).
9. You have come to me with lies and slanders (malicious falsehoods) in your mouths.
10. Leave your weeping, for it is of no avail (help, benefit) —and my time is short.

MULTIPLE CHOICE (1 pt. each)

1. How many of King Arthur's knights tried unsuccessfully to heal Sir Urry?
   - **a.** 100 knights
   - **b.** 110 knights
   - **c.** 120 knights
2. How did Launcelot free himself from Melliagraunce's dungeon?
   - **a.** He crosses himself
   - **b.** He fights the guards
   - **c.** He kisses the damsel
3. How many knights did King Arthur send to seize Launcelot in Guinevere's room?
   - **a.** 10 knights
   - **b.** 12 knights
   - **c.** 20 knights
4. Who advised Launcelot against visiting the queen in her room?
   - **a.** Sir Gawain
   - **b.** Sir Gareth
   - **c.** Sir Bors
5. Who ruled Britain in King Arthur's absence?
   - **a.** Launcelot
   - **b.** Bors
   - **c.** Mordred
6. To where did Guinevere escape from Mordred?
   - **a.** Tower of London
   - **b.** Avalon
   - **c.** Canterbury
7. Who warned King Arthur to make a truce with Mordred?
   - **a.** Gawain
   - **b.** Sir Bors
   - **c.** Launcelot
8. Why was King Arthur carried away in the barge?
   - **a.** so his wound would heal
   - **b.** to escape the Saxons
   - **c.** to escape Launcelot
9. After Launcelot's death, where do Hector and Bors go?
   - **a.** to Camelot
   - **b.** to France
   - **c.** to the Holy Land

QUOTATIONS (2 pts. each)

1. "Come out and fight, and all your treacherous curs with you—for here am I, Sir Launcelot of the Lake, ready to do battle with you all!"

   Who said it? Launcelot Where is he? He is outside Melliagraunce's castle.

2. "… here now you lie dying, the man whom I loved best in all the world. … For you and Launcelot I loved best of all my knights: and I have lost you both."

   Who said it? Arthur To whom? Gawain

3. "But be you sure that I will come again when the land of Britain has need of me, and the realm of Logres shall rise once more out of the darkness."

   Who said it? Arthur To whom? Sir Bedivere

COMPREHENSION QUESTIONS (3 pts. each)

1. What reminds King Arthur that Logres will soon fall?

   Launcelot heals Sir Urry. The Lady of the Lake had prophesied that when he healed someone again, Logres would soon pass.

2. What is Gawain's last request?

   He asks for forgiveness, and he requests that Launcelot return to Logres to fight for Arthur.

3. How does the battle with Mordred begin?

   Arthur is making peace with Mordred, but a soldier takes out his sword to kill a snake. Then both sides charge.

4. What do Guinevere and Launcelot do to repent of their sins?

   They each join a monastery.

King Arthur: Final Exam KEY

Name:______________________________ Date: ______________ Score: ________

135 total pts.

READING NOTES: Match each word below with the correct description. (1 pt. each)

Avalon	Camelot	Grail Priest	Logres	Tintagel
Balan	Castle Carbonek	Hector	Mordred	Uther Pendragon
Balyn	Elaine of Astolat	King Pant & Elayne	Naciens	
Bedivere	Enchanted Ship	Lady Liones	Saxons	
Blanchefleur	Excalibur	Lady Ragnell	Sir Bernlak	

1. Castle Carbonek place where the Holy Grail resides; place of the Dolorous Stroke

2. King Pant & Elayne king and queen of North Wales; parents of Launcelot

3. Balan brother of Balyn; the one Balyn loved most in the world

4. Saxons Germanic tribe that invaded Britain in the 5th & 6th centuries

5. Logres name of Arthur's kingdom

6. Camelot capital of Arthur's kingdom; modern-day Winchester, England

7. Excalibur the sword of Arthur

8. Uther Pendragon king of Briton; father of Arthur

9. Balyn knight who struck the Dolorous Stroke

10. Avalon Land of Mystery; place where Merlin took Arthur as an infant

11. Tintagel King Mark's castle in Cornwall; castle where Igrayne was tricked by Uther

12. Hector Launcelot's half-brother

13. Sir Bernlak Knight of the Lake; the Green Knight

14. Lady Liones sister of Lady Linnet; practices evil magic

15. Blanchefleur Percivale's love

16. Lady Ragnell under the curse of Morgana; marries Gawain

17. Elaine of Astolat daughter of King Pelles; in love with Launcelot

18. Naciens hermit who raised Galahad

19. Grail Priest Galahad

20. Enchanted Ship ship that takes Dindrane and the knights to their destination

21. Bedivere the only surviving knight to keep the legend of Logres alive

22. Mordred the most evil knight in Logres

VOCABULARY: Write the correct vocabulary word in the blanks below. (1 pt. each)

I 1. avail
N 2. ominous
J 3. slander
B 4. dissension
Q 5. renown
K 6. feeble
D 7. forsook
A 8. felon
M 9. hermit
P 10. vigil
O 11. dire
L 12. mortally
R 13. festered
C 14. fostered
F 15. scornfully
G 16. indistinct
H 17. wretched
E 18. succour

A. criminal, villain, lawbreaker
B. strife, conflict, disagreement
C. encouraged, nurtured
D. abandoned, deserted
E. to aid, assist, relieve
F. contemptuously, disdainfully
G. vague, hazy, murky
H. miserable, woeful
I. to help, benefit
J. malicious falsehood
K. weak, frail
L. fatally
M. one who lives in solitude
N. menacing, threatening
O. urgent, fearful
P. a watch, surveillance
Q. fame, celebrity
R. became infected, rotted

MULTIPLE CHOICE (1 pt. each)

1. King Arthur's foster father is:
- **a.** Sir Ector
- **b.** Sir Gawain
- **c.** Uther

2. Balan does not recognize Balyn because he does not have his own:
- **a.** shield
- **b.** sword
- **c.** armor

3. Merlin says the person who will bring about the downfall of Logres is:
- **a.** Launcelot
- **b.** Guinevere
- **c.** Morgana

4. The knight whose coming to the Round Table signifies one year before the Holy Grail comes is:
- **a.** Gawain
- **b.** Launcelot
- **c.** Percivale

5. The best knight of all will sit in the:
   a. Siege Perilous
   b. Siege Dangerous
   c. Siege Sinister
6. The Green Knight has come to Arthur's court to test the Round Table's:
   a. strength
   b. skill
   c. bravery
7. The person who sent the Green Knight to Arthur's court:
   a. Merlin
   b. Morgana
   c. Nimue
8. The chapel where Launcelot has to go to save the injured knight is the Chapel____________.
   a. Perilous
   b. Dangerous
   c. Dolorous
9. Sir Gareth's brother:
   a. Gawain
   b. Launcelot
   c. The Red Knight
10. The best knight Launcelot has ever jousted with:
    a. Gawain
    b. Percivale
    c. Tristram
11. To avenge the death of her brother, Queen Isaud keeps:
    a. a dragon's tooth
    b. a piece of a shirt
    c. a sword chip
12. Geraint goes to the hunt with:
    a. Guinevere
    b. Gawain
    c. Arthur
13. Oringle is:
    a. beheaded
    b. rewarded
    c. knighted
14. The mistress of the damsel who lures Arthur to Tarn Wathelyne:
    a. Nimue
    b. Allewes
    c. Morgana le Fay
15. Percivale does not see another living soul besides his mother until he is:
    a. 21
    b. 15
    c. 5
16. According to the damsel in the castle, the downfall of Logres will be caused by:
    a. Launcelot
    b. Gawain
    c. Percivale
17. The hermit who comes to Arthur's court predicts the birth of:
    a. Galahad
    b. Percivale
    c. Mordred
18. Launcelot cannot touch the Grail because of his:
    a. anger
    b. sin
    c. pride
19. Galahad was a descendant of:
    a. Joseph of Arimathea
    b. King Arthur
    c. Gawain
20. The unworthy knight who tries to take the golden crown:
    a. Launcelot
    b. Hector
    c. Melyas

21. Sir Lionel does penance for killing the monk for:
   a. 1 month + 1 day
   b. 6 months + 1 day
   c. 1 year + 1 day

22. The cure for the sick lady of the castle:
   a. the love of a pure knight
   b. blood from a pure virgin
   c. Galahad's arrival

23. Who was lying in the great hall at Castle Carbonek?
   a. Blanchefleur
   b. King Arthur
   c. King Pelles

24. Against whom did Naciens sin, which results in his long life?
   a. Merlin
   b. Nimue
   c. Joseph of Arimathea

25. Who joins Percivale and Blanchefleur in marriage?
   a. King Arthur
   b. Galahad
   c. King Pelles

26. How does Launcelot free himself from Melliagraunce's dungeon?
   a. He crosses himself.
   b. He fights the guards.
   c. He kisses the damsel.

27. Who advises Launcelot against visiting the queen in her room?
   a. Sir Gawain
   b. Sir Gareth
   c. Sir Bors

28. Who rules Britain in King Arthur's absence?
   a. Launcelot
   b. Bors
   c. Mordred

29. To where does Guinevere escape from Mordred?
   a. Tower of London
   b. Avalon
   c. Canterbury

30. After Launcelot's death, where do Hector and Bors go?
   a. to Camelot
   b. to France
   c. to the Holy Land

QUOTATIONS (2 pts. each)

1. "A little while after his birth at dark Tintagel, Uther, who hearkened to my words, gave the child into my care, and I bore him to Avalon, the Land of Mystery."

   Who said it? Merlin To whom? angry kings and knights

2. "Bury us, I pray you, in the same tomb, and write upon it that here lie two brothers who slew one another by mischance …"

   Who said it? Balan To whom? Lady of the Castle

3. "Yet I would that you loved another; for by her very beauty shall come the end of Logres."

   Who said it? Merlin To whom? Arthur

4. "A knight without mercy is dishonoured: but to kill a fair lady is shame unto the world's end!"

   Who said it? four armed knights To whom? Gawain

5. "For though I lack a weapon, yet shall I lack no honour—and if you slay me weaponless, it is you who will be shamed."

Who said it? Arthur To whom? Sir Accolon

6. "I have loved her long, and she me. And I promised to fight and slay whom she would, even though it were Arthur the King."

Who said it? Sir Accolon To whom? Arthur

7. "As for the lace, you hid it but for love of your life—and that is a little sin, and for it I pardon you."

Who said it? Sir Bernlak To whom? Gawain

8. "Merlin has spoken his name to you—and see, that name grows in letters of gold upon the empty siege on the right hand of the Siege Perilous!"

Who said it? Lady Nimue To whom? Arthur

9. "When you are a noble knight of noble birth, you shall have my love—but not before!"

Who said it? Lady Liones To whom? Sir Gareth

10. "Only Launcelot bowed his head in his hands, and the tears ran between his fingers as he thought of his own love for Guinevere."

Why does Launcelot cry? Launcelot cries because he knows exactly how Tristram feels.

11. "I have no lady. And yet … there is none fairer that ever I have seen than this damsel your daughter, the lady Enid … "

Who said it? Geraint To whom? Duke Liconal

12. "This is devil's work!"

When was this spoken? It was spoken when Arthur charged at Gromer Somer Joure.

13. "By this your choice—to leave the choice to me—you have undone the enchantment forever …"

Who said it? Ragnell To whom? Gawain

14. "In the days long past, Merlin the good enchanter told me that you would come when the highest moment of the realm of Logres drew near."

Who said it? Arthur To whom? Percivale

15. "Alas! I have lived too long, for now I am dishonoured!"

Who said it? Launcelot

16. "Sir, this is not my sword, nor am I worthy to wear it at my side. Evil shall come to any who seeks to draw it knowing that he is not worthy …"

Who said it? Launcelot To whom? Arthur

17. "Now blessed be the good fortune that brings this shield to me."

Who said it? Galahad To whom? the squire

18. "I give you my word that never again will I feel envy towards Sir Galahad."

Who said it? Percivale To whom? the hermit

19. "Go forward in the fear of God, and live to tell of the ending of the quest of the Holy Grail …"

Who said it? Naciens To whom? Sir Bors

20. "Alas, all my great deeds of arms have I done for the sake of Queen Guinevere, without stopping to think if they were right or wrong."

Who said it? Launcelot To whom? Naciens

21. "So shall the darkness fall upon Logres."

Who thought it? Gawain

What was he witnessing? He was witnessing a hand putting out the candles.

22. "And when he died, this penance was laid on me: that I should live beyond the span of mortal men to be the Priest of the Grail until the coming of Sir Galahad the Good Knight."

Who said it? Naciens To whom? Gawain

23. "Come out and fight, and all your treacherous curs with you—for here am I, Sir Launcelot of the Lake, ready to do battle with you all!"

Who said it? Launcelot Where was he? He was outside Melliagraunce's castle.

24. "… here now you lie dying, the man whom I loved best in all the world. … For you and Launcelot I loved best of all my knights: and I have lost you both."

Who said it? Arthur To whom? Gawain

25. "But be you sure that I will come again when the land of Britain has need of me, and the realm of Logres shall rise once more out of the darkness."

Who said it? Arthur To whom? Sir Bedivere

ESSAY (15 pts.)

Describe Launcelot's struggle with good and evil. This should include the cause of his struggle, his attempts to live a virtuous life, his failures, and their consequences.

Essays should have some of these major points:

Launcelot was a brave and chivalrous knight. Knights who abided by the code of chivalry were generally virtuous to the degree that they were successful. Launcelot, however, failed to recognize that rules must be kept which were not in the code. Two rules which he disobeyed were: to be loyal and obedient to your lord, and to not commit adultery. Although it was quite honorable for Launcelot to idealize a married woman as the paragon of virtue, he let his respect for her turn into romantic love. Even then, he could have controlled himself, yet he succumbed to his desires and revealed his moral weakness. This resulted in his inability to seize the Grail when it descended. It ultimately led to the end of Logres.